#FollowTheLeader

Lessons in Social Media Success from #HigherEd CEOs

#FollowTheLeader

Lessons in Social Media Success from #HigherEd CEOs

A book by Dan Zaiontz, MCM

EDUniverse Media
St Louis, MO

Project Manager: Jennifer Presley
Copy Editor: Robin Netherton
Designer: Mike Schulz
Cover Design: Mike Schulz, Sarah Eva Monroe

The cover text and interior text is Roboto.

Published by EDUniverse Media, St. Louis, Missouri. EDUniverse Media is a division of mStoner, Inc.

Library of Congress Cataloging-in-Publication Data

ISBN (pbk): 978-0-9888788-2-2 ISBN (ebk): 978-0-9888788-3-9

DEDICATION

For Rebecca, Mom, Dad, Keren, and Adina, you have always shown unwavering faith in my abilities and encouraged me to challenge my fears. So, hold on to your butts. And for my daughter, Samantha, this is proof that neat things happen when you try your best.

ACKNOWLEDGEMENTS

I firmly believe that there is no journey in life without a lesson to be learned. The writing of this book has itself been a journey with a multitude of lessons. I have learned that almost any challenge is surmountable when one is committed to overcoming it. I have learned that if we let fear dictate our actions, we risk never fulfilling the entirety of our potential. And most importantly, I have learned that a few very special people in our lives can help to shape our destinies, teaching us lessons whose value we may not immediately realize.

For me, those special people are members of my family and friends; the McMaster–Syracuse MCM community, including students, alumni, and faculty, such as Michael Meath, Dr. Laurence Mussio, Dr. Alex Sévigny, and Dr. Terry Flynn; my colleague Michael Stoner (and his associates); editor Robin Netherton; and my fellow staff members at Seneca College. Without support from each of these individuals, this book would never have come to pass, nor would I have even persisted through the accompanying crises of confidence or pounced on the periods of inspiration.

I offer my sincere thanks to the 22 Canadian and American college and university presidents who served as my research participants in spring 2013, despite demanding schedules and numerous other pressing priorities. Your insights will help to shape future decision-making at the most senior levels of global higher education.

And finally, I owe special words of gratitude to my wife, Rebecca, and my mom, Lucy. They have helped me to redefine what I once believed to be possible. A million thank-yous wouldn't cover it.

TABLE OF CONTENTS

INTRODUCTION

I can tell you the exact moment it occurred to me to start writing about higher ed leaders who were active on social media. It was Feb. 1, 2013, at 2:50 p.m.

In winter 2013, I was approaching the completion of my Master of Communications Management degree from McMaster University–Syracuse University, and I began to think about a thesis topic. Simultaneously, in my day job at Toronto's Seneca College of Applied Arts & Technology, I was researching social media policies at postsecondary institutions. And I came across the name of Dr. Santa Ono, president of the University of Cincinnati.

Dr. Ono's name had appeared high up in search results under the keywords "higher education," "social media," "leadership," and "policy." But it wasn't until 2:50 p.m. that I paid much attention. Then, I opened a Google Alert with a link to an article in Cincinnati Magazine, titled #PrezOnBoard. Its subhead read: "Even before trustees tapped him as the school's new president, Santa Ono was a campus rock star. But does the tweeting, Bearcat-loving, Ivy League–trained scientist have what it takes to lead the University of Cincinnati into the big leagues?"

The lead continued, "As the University of Cincinnati played football against Rutgers on November 17, a circle of UC cheerleaders hoisted the school's new president, Santa Ono, aloft on the sidelines of Nippert Stadium. Clad in a red blazer, surrounded by rustling pom-poms, Ono waved to the crowd as the crowd cheered back. "Does your president do this?" one student tweeted, shooting a photo of the antics out to her followers. "I didn't think so." It wasn't a one-off moment for Ono—he is all over Twitter, relentlessly selling UC to itself and the world outside."

That day, I began to follow President Ono on Twitter. I quickly learned that he'd developed a dynamic and active social media presence and was promoting his university with the #HottestCollegeInAmerica hashtag. Through his account, Ono engaged with current and prospective students, celebrated institutional achievements, shared stories from his personal and professional life, and addressed questions and concerns of internal and external stakeholders.

I was hooked. I loved the way this 50-year-old, transplanted Canadian scientist-turned-president approached his social media presence. Dr. Ono's Twitter presence struck me as an example of social media's power to help a higher ed leader to boost his own reputation and that of his institution, to communicate and engage directly and effectively with stakeholders on a platform of their choosing, to set a standard for customer relationship management for the institution, and to reach new audiences with key messages and announcements from and about the institution. In short: This was the perfect topic for my thesis.

In the months that followed, I began researching the academic and business literature that existed on social media best practices for organizational leaders. I began following more higher ed leaders—specifically, Canadian and American college and university presidents—on Twitter and other social networks, to observe their day-to-day activities. I wanted to better understand how strategic advisers and professional communicators could support senior leaders in their social media activities, applying their inherent familiarity with stakeholder engagement, media relations, and reputation and relationship management. And I decided that my thesis would focus on helping senior leaders and public relations professionals alike to better collaborate to advance strategic interests.

As the project moved forward, I started cold-calling higher ed leaders across North America. And I took to Twitter to invite many of them to chat about their social media approaches, best practices, advice, and warnings about the potential risks. More than 20 of them agreed to be confidentially interviewed as part of my research. Many of their insights formed the foundation for the recommendations found in this book.

My conversations with the college and university presidents covered a variety of issues. For example, I learned their perspectives on the opportunities and risks of putting yourself, as a president, out there on social media. I heard stories about how these tools could be applied in ways that had a significant impact on institutional reputations and results. I learned that higher ed leaders could strategically operate their personal and professional social media accounts. I discovered what counsel they wished to receive from their strategic advisers and how it could help them enhance their engagement on social media. And I listened to them discuss how a president could keep institutional interests and key messages front and center in social media channels.

One of my primary observations is that because presidents differ in their personalities and objectives, there's no one formula or prescription for success on social media. And even though many presidents are succeeding in their embrace of social media, the presidents I spoke to were very clear that social media was not a platform for every higher ed leader, particularly those who considered themselves risk-averse.

In November 2013, I defended my thesis, titled "#FollowTheLeader: A Study of Best Practices in Social Media Use by University and College Presidents in Canada and the United States," in front of about 100 colleagues, family, and friends. The defense was also live-streamed, live-tweeted, and viewed by about 1,500 strangers around the world, one of whom was Michael Stoner, president of mStoner, Inc. Michael believed that *#FollowTheLeader* offered salient insights to higher ed leaders and their advisers and proposed that I excerpt portions of my thesis for this book.

We intend *FollowTheLeader: Lessons in Social Media Success from #HigherEd CEOs* to be a resource for senior executives who wish to enhance their own and their institution's presence on social networks and advance personal, professional, and institutional priorities.

Throughout the book, you'll find profiles of higher ed leaders who use social media to strengthen strategic relationships with students, faculty, media, volunteers, government officials, and alumni. Some chapters were specifically requested by individual presidents: Chapter 5 on why a one-size-fits-all approach to social media cannot work for many college and university presidents, Chapter 7 on establishing your social media rules of engagement, Chapter 9 on recommendations for personal social media strategies, and Chapter 10 on the importance of committing to your social media engagement. At the end of each chapter, you'll also find handy summaries for strategic advisers and the presidents themselves, labeled respectively as "Strategic adviser's share" and "President's post."

I can't guarantee that following the steps in this book will forever change the trajectory of a college president's career or help an institution make its way to the top of a national ranking. What this book will show you is that Canadian and American college and university presidents are using social media to change the nature, role, and expectations of their positions. In the minds of some of these presidents, the future holds more—and not less— of this change. As one of the American presidents I interviewed said, "To not come in with a social media tool in your tool belt means that you're less able than you would be otherwise. Why would one choose to be there?"

Before Going Social

Chapter 1

—

#PersonalChoice

Throughout my many conversations with CEOs, presidents, and organizational senior leaders on the topic of engaging on social media, the question of necessity has often come up, and the consensus position to date has been, quite honestly, that social media use isn't essential. At least, not yet.

This might sound like a counterintuitive point with which to open a book on social media best practices, but it's undoubtedly important. Many of us have heard the social media penetration metrics, particularly the ones most relevant to higher education leadership. According to the 2013 Pew Research Internet Project, 83 percent of 18- to 29-year-olds, a key demographic group for universities and colleges, were active users of social media, and 73 percent of all adults online were regular visitors of social networking sites. And those numbers are only trending upward.

Increasingly, college and university presidents are taking note of the strategic opportunities presented by engaging with stakeholders on these networks. According to a 2013 study out of the University of Massachusetts Dartmouth Center for Marketing Research, more than half of American college presidents maintain an active presence on Facebook and Twitter, beating the number of Fortune 500 CEOs active on social media by more than 20 percent. If the numbers are telling us that more than half of American higher ed leadership is active on social media, then why argue that it isn't an essential communications tool in the toolbox of a college president?

In spite of the numbers, the question of whether to have a presence on social media in one's capacity as president of a college or university is very much a personal choice, with no clear right or wrong answer. Many of the social-media-active presidents I interviewed as part of my research took this stance, and I happen to agree with them. Right now, we do not live in a world where a college or university president's presence on social media is a must. If you are a senior leader who believes that (a) neither you nor your institution can benefit from your presence on a social network; (b) your communications style and personality are not suited to the two-way, fast-paced conversational nature of many social networks; (c) your busy schedule will limit your ability to maintain a consistent, organic, and conversational presence on whichever social network you choose; and/or (d) thoughtful and meaningful conversations cannot take place on social media, then who is to say that you should ignore your instincts?

In fact, if you are a higher ed senior executive who holds any of these beliefs, I would advise you not to pursue the creation of a social media presence, because in all likelihood it will do more harm than good to your personal, professional, and institutional reputations. Don't let anyone tell you that you have to be on social media, particularly if you have studied all the facts and come to believe that it's not for you.

In February 2013, former University of British Columbia (UBC) President Stephen Toope told his institution's student newspaper, the *Ubyssey*, what he really thought about Twitter. "Twitter is the epitome of the immediate reaction dynamic present in too much social media," he told the publication. "Given the short messages, and the ease of re-transmission, Twitter encourages thoughtless, reactive modes of communication." The UBC president's position was that society's continued reliance on Twitter (and platforms like it) could lead to a deterioration of intellectual discourse. Toope's criticisms of social media engagement stemmed from his belief that the level of discourse on Twitter, given its limitation of 140 characters per message, was not sufficient to deliver substantive messages and engage in meaningful conversations. Toope's comments garnered strong reactions from social media detractors and supporters alike in British Columbia and across Canada. Those who agreed with Toope believed social media use was harming our collective ability to have thoughtful conversations, while those who disagreed with Toope considered his critique to be unfounded and lacking in specificity as well as credible examples.

From my perspective, Toope's comments conveniently ignore the millions of social networking users who engage in daily conversations about complex, relevant, and meaningful subjects, including certain higher ed leaders who use these tools to discuss policy issues tied to their sector. The UBC president's stated viewpoint is still prominently held by a number of his counterparts who are unfamiliar with how some of their colleagues are using social media to engage in meaningful and institutionally beneficial conversations.

So, would I advise someone like President Toope with a philosophical opposition to social media to give it a try anyway? I might—if I felt the individual in question hadn't taken the time to ask some valuable questions and gather some important information.

DECIDING FACTORS AND IMPORTANT QUESTIONS

Before completely rejecting or embracing these tools, college and university presidents must be certain they have in fact considered all the information available to them and asked the right questions.

- Have you studied how other higher ed leaders are employing social media tools? What are their reasons for engaging with stakeholders through these platforms and channels? What have they achieved through this engagement?

- Have you consulted with your strategic advisers to truly evaluate the risks and opportunities of social media engagement? Have you assessed your personal capacity for risk, say, if your conversations on social media happen to spin out of control or veer into negative territory?

- Have you determined which social network or networks you might choose and which of these networks optimally aligns with your strengths as a communicator?

- Outside of social media, have you embraced other ways of directly connecting with your most valued stakeholders, either in person or otherwise, that enables you to gather intelligence and critical feedback on the strengths and weaknesses of your institution? Have you found other methods through which to track, promote, and keep abreast of higher ed thought leadership, trends, and emerging issues?

If you can confidently respond to each of these questions without seeing a fit for social media in your mandate as president, then the choice for you is a simple one: Buck the numbers and keep doing what you're doing.

However, many college and university presidents have chosen otherwise. A presence on Facebook, Twitter, Google+, Instagram, Vine, or another social network has helped them to advance any number of professional and/or institutional interests. According to my research, higher ed leaders are using social media to engage with prospective and current students, faculty, alumni, government, media, and fundraising stakeholders, in some cases enhancing those relationships for the purposes of advancing strategic agendas. Those same leaders are actively listening to their campus communities through social media, identifying the issues most important to them, and taking action on those issues quickly and decisively, earning them, as one American university president put it, "political capital on their campuses." Some leaders are using their presence on social media to celebrate the achievements of their institution, develop their own professional reputation, or gain a better understanding of what their competition is up to. Their objectives may be personal to each user, but many presidents have found value in social media that other forms of communication may not offer them, particularly given their often busy schedules.

Some of the presidents I spoke to talked about the fact that when they were in meetings off campus or traveling on institutional business, social media was their optimal means by which to stay engaged with their campus community and valued stakeholders. Because almost every social media platform can be accessed using mobile technology, presidents appreciated the fact that they could "check in" with their institution wherever they happened to be. Other presidents carved out brief segments of their day to dedicate to social media engagement to ensure they delivered consistent content to their followers and promptly responded to inquiries.

WEIGH THE COSTS AND BENEFITS

It is important to recognize that an informed choice on whether a higher ed leader should be active on social media can take place only after a thorough cost-benefit analysis of the risks and opportunities has been completed. Many of the presidents who have abstained from entering the social media space have done so because their version of the cost-benefit calculation just didn't add up. In their view, the risk of a public misstep was too great. The potential gains or advancement of institutional interests were not significant enough or sufficiently measurable. They felt their institutional social media accounts were effective enough for the two-way communication efforts of their colleges or universities. They believed there simply wasn't a demand from stakeholders to hear from and engage with them, or they couldn't find a way to fit social media into their busy lives. There also remains a segment of higher ed leaders who believe that social media channels, due to their instantaneous and sometimes anonymous nature, in some ways degrade thoughtful discourse rather than enhancing it. They contend that social media is simply a fad and ask themselves why they should invest their time and resources into a technological platform that could go the way of MySpace at any moment, especially when they have so much else on their plates.

Each of these concerns is perfectly valid. If a college president, after thoroughly researching the costs and benefits of social media engagement, still holds some or all of these beliefs, then he or she is best served by staying off of it altogether. But I would argue that for most higher ed leaders, a thorough cost-benefit analysis will convince them not to avoid social media but to embrace it. On the issue of risk of a public misstep on social media, a number of college presidents told me that there was risk in every communication activity that they were involved with, and that embracing risk is simply part of the job. On the matter of measurable gains from social media, several presidents told me stories of renewed funding, strategically aligned legislative change, strengthened relationships, improved student satisfaction metrics, and increased reputational perceptions about their institution stemming from their social media activities. On the topic of institutional social media accounts serving the same purpose as presidential ones, many of the presidents I spoke to told me that their personal account was able to set the tone for their institution in terms of a commitment to customer service while also serving as a beacon to stakeholders, telling them "our door is always open, and we're readily accessible." With regard to audiences not wanting to hear from them, the social-media-active presidents told me the response to their engagement was almost entirely positive. Students, faculty, staff, and other stakeholders welcomed their arrival, interactions, and social media content and saw their presence as being separate and distinct from that of the institutional social media account. As for the issue of the degradation of thoughtful discourse, the presidents I interviewed endeavored to set an example on social media by ensuring that their content and discussions were thoughtful and strategic and reflected well on their institution. Finally, on the charge that social media is simply a fad best to be avoided, many of the presidents I spoke to paralleled such beliefs to the early critics of the telephone, television, email, and internet, who eventually proved themselves to be out of touch.

#YOUROWNCHOICE

The question of whether a higher ed leader ought to choose to engage on social media will always be a personal choice, no matter the arguments for or against. No one else—neither a strategic adviser, a well-intentioned author, nor a consultant—can make a decision like that on behalf of a college or university president. But while the choice has to be a personal one, it doesn't have to be irrevocable.

Perhaps the one best way to assess whether social media engagement is meant for you is to try it. Almost every social network that a higher ed leader might consider offers the functionality to create an account for free. Experiment with an anonymous account; lurk around and see what conversations are taking place about your institution. Explore what content is gaining traction, and monitor what your counterparts are doing well and not so well. If, after this foray into the space, you continue to feel that there is no place for you on social media, simply delete your anonymous account and move on to the other multiple priorities on your plate. However, if you believe there is substance to the points I've raised in this chapter and the views expressed by social-media-active higher ed leaders, and value in the engagement you've witnessed for yourself on social media, then make the choice to put yourself out there. You just might find benefits you hadn't previously considered—and even greater value if you read the remainder of this book.

STRATEGIC ADVISER'S SHARE

• Work with your president to help him determine whether a presence on social media is right for him. Offer him an environmental scan of the social media landscape as it might relate to him. Ask yourself: Which of his competitors have an active presence on social media? On which social networks do they operate? Do the accounts appear to be operated by the presidents themselves or by staff from the Office of the President? What kind of content are they sharing through their accounts, and what sorts of conversations are they engaging in? What value might your president and the institution gain from an active presence on social media? What risks might he face? What institutional interests could a potential presidential account serve to advance?

• Once you've presented all the information to your president, the decision is in her hands. Wherever she lands, respect her decision. It's neither right nor wrong. It's personal. And, it's not irrevocable. Social media isn't going away.

PRESIDENT'S POST

• Either independently or with the help of a strategic adviser, research the social media landscape around you. You may begin your investigation by creating an anonymous account with which to lurk on various social networks. Ask yourself: Who are the major higher ed players (e.g. other college and university presidents) or leaders you admire outside of higher education? What are they using their social media accounts for? What do they do most effectively and least effectively, in your estimation? How are their social media activities strategically supporting their institutional interests? Which social media platforms best suit your communications style? What are the major issues being discussed tied to your institution on social media, and how could your presence in those discussions alter the outcome, for either better or worse?

• If your own research or the work of your adviser has led you to consider testing the social media waters, then work with the adviser or your communications team to develop a president's social media strategy (see Chapter 9) before launching your publicly accessible account.

- If your social media research or cost-benefit analysis has led you to believe that a presidential social media account would not be of value to you, I respect your decision. There is no right or wrong answer here. It's a personal choice, and it certainly isn't irrevocable. I just hope that yours reflects an informed cost-benefit analysis.

Chapter 2

—

#AreYouFeelingLucky

Much in the same way your assessment of social media's costs and benefits depends on factors personal to you—such as how the technology might align with your communication style and how it might fit into your busy life—so does your assessment of the risks social media engagement presents. Those risks, along with an understanding of your own aversion to risk, are important considerations when weighing whether social media is for you.

As a university or college president, you must assess your personal capacity for tolerating risk before venturing into the social media space. Failing to honestly evaluate your personal level of risk aversion could leave you unprepared for the volatility of social networks and the potential for reputationally damaging experiences while engaging within the space.

According to the presidents I spoke to, the biggest risk they had to weigh before jumping in to social media was the potential to damage their personal, professional, and institutional reputations by making a public misstep or saying the wrong thing. Others were concerned about their personal security, in the event that someone with malicious intentions was tracking their movements and activities on social media. There were also fears that social media accounts might be hacked, and inappropriate or damaging content spread through those compromised accounts; that a president's social media activity might be misperceived; and that misunderstandings over social media messages might alienate key stakeholders. Many of these concerns are completely legitimate, and a number of higher ed leaders globally have already experienced such misfortunes. Yet many of those same leaders remain active on social media despite these challenges because they understand that embracing a certain amount of risk is part of the reality of being a social-media-active president and that risk in general simply comes with the territory of the presidential role. However, if you are unwilling to embrace some of the risks associated with social media engagement, then you would be better off finding other communications channels to pursue.

Still, just because social media engagement comes with its fair share of risks for college and university presidents, that doesn't mean that some of those risks can't be mitigated to some extent. In this chapter, we'll take a look at some of the risks of social media and what higher ed leaders can do to protect themselves from those risks.

PUBLIC MISSTEPS

College and university presidents fear making public missteps in their social media updates, messages, and engagement—that is, saying something they might regret or that could harm their own or their institution's reputation.

For example, in January 2013, former Louisiana College (LC) President Joe Aguillard posted a controversial article regarding the college's position on the "issue of Calvinism" to his "President's Pen" blog, a space "dedicated to making clear that trumpet sound of this President's position on where [he] stand[s] in relation to leading Louisiana College." LC is a private Baptist-affiliated institution based in Pineville, Louisiana, but neither students nor faculty are required to be members of that denomination to attend or be employed by the college. Aguillard, whose presidential tenure was laden with controversial moments, argued in the blog post that his was not a "hyper-Calvinist" institution. Reaction on social media and in the blogosphere was strong and swift, putting Aguillard on the defensive and forcing him and his administration to address the comments. Later in 2014, when the LC board removed Aguillard from his position as president (for reasons not officially related to the blog), one member of the local media argued that the blog post was the catalyst for the decision. Should Aguillard have chosen social media as his platform through which to broach issues of religion on campus? I'd argue, probably not.

Meanwhile, Ellie Ashford of the American Association of Community Colleges wrote in August 2013 about a minor social media controversy faced by Harrisburg (Pa.) Area Community College President John "Ski" Sygielski, an active user of Twitter, Facebook, and LinkedIn who also blogs. Sygielski "received a complaint from a parent who objected to a tweet about a gay and lesbian issue, even though [Sygielski] didn't express a viewpoint." However, after a follow-up conversation with the parent in question, the president was able to clear up the misunderstanding by providing context, clarity, and background to his initial 140-character message.

The best strategies to avoid public missteps, according to the presidents I spoke to, are mostly matters of common sense: Evaluate whether you would be comfortable with the social media content you were creating appearing on the front page of a newspaper or newscast the next day; give every social media update a sober second thought; avoid heated or complex discussions on microblogging platforms like Twitter where character limits can often detract from context; and endeavor to maintain a positive and upbeat tone in all your social media conversations. To that list, I would also add this: Ask yourself whether the message you are delivering aligns with the strategic interests and organizational values of your institution. If your message doesn't align with your interests or values, it would be probably not make sense for you to publish those thoughts on social media. While these solutions are not cure-alls for avoiding social media missteps completely, they may help to reduce your concerns about this perceived risk that comes with social engagement.

In the tweet below, President Paul LeBlanc (@SNHUPrez) of Southern New Hampshire University deftly handles what could have been a negative exchange with a student:

Cait Brown @caitbrown333: @snhuprez Love that we're growing our campus with a new dorm, but anyway we can start construction a little bit later? We need some sleep

> **Paul LeBlanc** @snhuprez: @CaitBrown333 But this is a great way to get an early start on homework and greet the day! Think of it as a very big alarm clock.

PERSONAL SECURITY

Many higher ed leaders are also concerned that actively engaging on social media might pose risks to their personal security. These perceived risks might involve some kind of criminal element tracking your movements on social media in order to harm you or your family, or someone with malicious intent attempting to secure private information about you through your social media account, without your consent.

Once again, the higher ed leaders I interviewed offered relatively common-sense advice on addressing these fears. Do not share personal details on social media that, in your assessment, could harm either you or your family. If you do not wish for your whereabouts to be tracked, then don't post about where you are and how long you'll be there. If you wish for certain private information about yourself to remain private, then keep that information off of social media. Higher ed leaders can avoid most threats to personal security resulting from social media engagement by simply not sharing information they fear falling into the wrong hands.

Documented cases of higher ed leaders facing personal security issues on social media are few and far between, but the fear is something many public figures must grapple with. Somewhat unavoidably, the meeting and travel schedules of certain college and university presidents are a matter of public record, which can present the same kind of perceived security threat as sharing one's movements through social media. However, in the case of social media, a president at least has the choice about which movements to share.

If you or your family members are particularly concerned about the issue of social media jeopardizing your personal security, it is important for you and your strategic advisers to take steps to address those concerns. You could, for instance, decide not to share social media updates relating to out-of-town travels and stick primarily to thought leadership content, or you might decide never to share information about your spouse, children or immediate family through the presidential account. These decisions are part of establishing your social media rules of engagement and your social media strategy, matters I discuss in greater depth in Chapters 7 and 9, respectively.

FAKE OR HACKED ACCOUNTS

"Dreading going into work tomorrow, but those diplomas aren't going to sign themselves..."

Tweet from 2009 emanating from a fake account impersonating University of Texas at Austin President William Powers.

While social media can enable senior executives to connect with diverse audiences, it also puts them at greater risk of being targeted by individuals using those platforms for malicious purposes. As I conducted my research, I found several cases of American higher ed leaders who were being impersonated on social media by people seeking to damage the reputations of those presidents or their institutions. In 2011, Steve Kolowich of *USA Today* wrote a piece outlining the challenges that some higher ed presidents were experiencing at that time with imposters on social media. "In the last two years, fake presidential Twitter accounts have cropped up at Columbia University, Wesleyan University, Georgetown University, Brown University, the University of Texas at Austin, and Vassar College," he wrote. A related problem is the threat of a hacked account, in which someone with malicious intentions gains access to your username and password and begins posting on your behalf. Both fake accounts and hacked accounts have been used to spread damaging messages about the presidents themselves or their institutions.

Although there is no easy fix for repairing the damage caused by a fake or hacked account, there are steps higher ed leaders can take to ensure they are not the victim of an imposter or hacker.

Social networks like Twitter and Facebook have attempted to combat the creation of fake accounts by offering a special "verified" account status to celebrities, government officials, and other public figures who request it because theirs are most often the accounts targeted by impersonators. Securing a verified badge on your social media profile can help followers to separate the real account from a fake one.

Next, either independently or with the support of your staff, regularly and actively search for social media profiles that may be impersonating you. You can do this by searching for your name or title or variations of both (e.g. your username with an underscore at the end) on whichever social network you are using (as well as those you may not be active on) to ensure yours is the only result that shows up.

To avoid your account being hacked, it is important to consistently change your account password. In addition, choosing a complex password (e.g. with symbols, numbers, and capital letters) to begin with will make it more difficult for anyone to break into your account.

If your social media account has been hacked or impersonated, contact the account security team of the social network you are using, as instructed in the "Help" section of the platform's official website. Social networks care about ensuring their users have a positive experience, so they will usually be quick in assisting you. They will likely ask for proof of your identity (e.g. a scanned copy of your driver's license or passport) as well as the user-name of the impersonating account. Some presidents dealing with faked or hacked accounts also take to social media in return to set the record straight and communicate correct information to followers.

If despite your best efforts, your account continues to be hacked, or if an impersonating account isn't shut down by the network, work with your strategic advisers and communications staff to develop a plan to address the situation.

In 2009, President John DeGioia of Georgetown University and President William Powers of the University of Texas at Austin both faced issues and delays when they requested that imposter accounts be shut down by Twitter. In the years since those incidents, however, the now—publicly traded social network, recognizing the damage that fake accounts can cause, has developed policies to make such requests easier.

In the case of a hacked account, presidents may consider taking the dramatic step of deleting the account if a password change fails to resolve the security breach. That plan might also call for posting a message informing your followers that you've created an alternate account, or it could involve issuing a statement to internal and external stakeholders to inform them of the issue.

Whatever your response, the quicker you and your team are at addressing the matter and providing followers with accurate information, the easier it will be to limit the damage.

ALTERED PERCEPTIONS

Higher ed leaders also face the risk of professional repercussions as a result of their social media activities.

John Maeda, named the president of the Rhode Island School of Design (RISD) in 2008, was recognized by staff, faculty, students, and administration alike as having advanced social media acumen, supported by his substantial following of more than 175,000 Twitter users. However, staff and faculty at RISD were not happy with Maeda's leadership style, which was perceived to emphasize and encourage social media engagement above all other forms, including in-person interaction. There were also concerns about Maeda's fundraising results and his ability to manage faculty relations. In a 2011 article about Maeda's difficulties in *The Chronicle of Higher Education*, Jeffrey Young wrote, "Many professors at the art school do not appreciate being part of Mr. Maeda's high-tech experiment in leadership." Young observed that while Maeda excelled at engaging with stakeholders using social media tools, he was unable to communicate with the same level of effectiveness in other ways. In March of that year, more than 80 percent of the RISD faculty voted "no confidence" in the president's performance. Social media was part of the problem. To staff and faculty, Maeda's excessive tweeting felt more like a distraction, and his overt focus on social media engagement called into question his progress on other institutional priorities. Maeda was primarily criticized for being unable to convey his vision for leadership outside of new media platforms, and that perception nearly led to the termination of his presidency.

Higher ed leaders must seriously evaluate how their social media usage could be perceived by internal stakeholders. Too much time devoted to social media engagement ahead of other forms of professional interaction, such as in-person meetings or attendance at institutional events, or other presidential responsibilities, such as fundraising, could be viewed as a misappropriation of priorities and resources by that leader. Effective social media engagement by a higher ed leader cannot be considered a kind of panacea replacing other forms of communication expected of a college or university president. Such perceptions can be addressed by treating social media as a tool with which to complement and not replace the other available communications options.

ALIENATING KEY RELATIONSHIPS

College and university presidents also fear alienating key stakeholders—students, faculty, staff, alumni, government officials, donors, partners, or media—through their social media engagement. By wading into contentious issues or expressing controversial opinions, leaders can offend stakeholders or damage perceptions, which in turn undermines their ability to do their job effectively. This fear is completely understandable given that in the 21st century, the biggest part of a president's job is managing strategic internal and external relationships. Add to that, the opportunity to engage with key stakeholders and strengthen those relationships is one of the elements that draws so many higher ed leaders onto social media in the first place. Alienation of important stakeholder relationships is mostly avoidable by once again following some rather obvious advice.

Presidents can avoid alienating stakeholder relationships by consistently offering content that appeals to their stakeholders and keeping engagement with those stakeholders positive and helpful. Social-media-active presidents are masters of ensuring the content they share is relevant to the stakeholder groups with which they communicate. They stay in that zone and don't often diverge from it.

Actively listening to one's audiences can also help steer a higher ed leader in the right direction with respect to optimal content to share and engagement to pursue. In the tweet below, an alumna of the University of Missouri (MU) shares feedback about content she appreciates receiving from MU Chancellor R. Bowen Loftin:

Stacey @bonedvm: @bowtieger Love the weekly chancellor updates! Thanks for including us alumni!!

Presidents who disregard such feedback from their social media followers are most likely to offer them irrelevant content and alienate these valuable relationships.

OTHER COMMON FEARS

The presidents I spoke to shared some additional concerns about their social media engagement. Some worried that they might choose a social media tool that could fall out of favor in a matter of months, like MySpace or Friendster. Others feared devoting time to social media engagement with little to show for it, in the end, in terms of results gained for themselves or their institutions. Lastly, some presidents were afraid that they might be unable to attract followers, meaning that their engagement would fail to reach key stakeholders and represent a waste of time, effort, and resources. While these concerns are legitimate and real, a higher ed leader must assess whether the potential gains outweigh the perceived risks. I briefly address some of these fears (and how to mitigate them) below as well as later in the book.

Strategies to avoid choosing the wrong tool might include identifying social networks in which higher ed leaders are firmly entrenched and established with a strong track record of success (e.g. Twitter, Facebook, YouTube, LinkedIn, and blogs) and choosing a social media platform based on your stated goals or objectives. If you are looking to reach student, faculty, alumni, government, and media stakeholders in order to strengthen ties with those groups, Twitter could be an option to consider. If you want to engage with your colleagues for professional development purposes, LinkedIn might be your best bet. In Chapter 4, I break down the major social networks a college or university president might consider and analyze the pros and cons of each option.

Presidents can avoid wasting time on social media by developing a social media strategy and tactics calendar (see Chapter 9) so that their engagement and activities align with their personal, professional, or institutional goals. When you approach your social media engagement with a strategic plan and measurable goals, you can ensure that your activities are not aimless and random but rather targeted and meaningful.

Higher ed leaders can avoid being left without followers by employing strategies used by other successful college and university presidents on social media and by cross-promoting their account through their campus's institutional profile. While numbers of followers and "likes" were at one time used as measures of success on social media, many marketers now argue that too much emphasis is placed on such metrics. Higher ed leaders should, alternatively, concern themselves with how their social media activities are moving the proverbial needles that are important to their institution. I discuss this further in Chapter 8, where we break down what metrics presidents might be better off measuring other than how many followers they have.

#YOUROWNCHOICE

In the end, the decision about whether you believe the risks inherent in social media engagement are surmountable are tied to your personal philosophy on risk aversion. You can talk to your fellow higher ed leaders who are active on social media, and they can share their views on the subject, but they can't make the decision for you. (For further discussion of the risks involved in social media use, see #RisksAndRewards in the Bonus Material at the end of this book.)

If few or none of the proposed strategies referenced above have quelled the apprehension you may feel about engaging on social media, then perhaps it isn't the communications vehicle you should pursue. However, it is important to note that there truly is no communications activity that is completely free of risk, and this chapter proves that the risks associated with social media engagement can mostly be mitigated. So, the question is, are you the kind of higher ed leader who embraces measured risk for the chance at potentially significant rewards? Only you can answer that.

STRATEGIC ADVISER'S SHARE

- You can help your president assess her aversion to risk by helping her to create a list of her biggest social media fears. Then, propose strategies to mitigate or address those fears.

- Respect your president's position if, after weighing the risks and proposed solutions, he feels unsuited for or uninterested in engaging on social media.

PRESIDENT'S POST

- Honestly evaluate your personal capacity for tolerating risk before venturing onto social media.

- Have a frank conversation with your strategic advisers or counterparts about your biggest social media fears and any risks you perceive to be keeping you from embracing the tools. Are there strategies you can employ to address these risks? What strategies do other higher ed leaders use to manage risk on social media?

- As part of your social media strategy, develop a risk management plan to address your biggest areas of concern and the procedures you will institute to overcome those issues.

SOCIAL PROFILE: @BOWTIEGER

Dr. R. Bowen Loftin, Chancellor, University of Missouri (former President of Texas A&M University)

BIO IN BRIEF

- Became chancellor of the University of Missouri (MU) in Columbia, Missouri on 1 February, 2014
- Served as president of Texas A & M University in College Station, Texas, from 2010 to 2014
- Professor of physics at MU
- Citations and honors include the University of Houston - Downtown Awards for Excellence in Teaching and in Service (twice), the American Association of Artificial Intelligence Award for an innovative application of artificial intelligence, NASA's Space Act Award, the NASA Public Service Medal, the NASA Invention of the Year Award (1995), the IEEE Computer Society's Meritorious Service Award (2005), and the IEEE Virtual Reality Conference Career Award (2008)
- Currently active on Twitter, Facebook, Google+, LinkedIn, YouTube

Source: University of Missouri's Office of the Chancellor website (http://chancellor.missouri.edu/biography/)

SOCIAL QUOTES

On the rewards of social media: "My joy every day is not in paperwork or endless meetings or making hard decisions, it's in interaction with students. Period. And I can only achieve that in an appreciable way with social media."

On risk management: "My job is often about risk management ... I know how to manage risk, and I manage my risk on social media by being very alert and very careful and cautious about what I put out there. But what outweighs the risk is that I can monitor it to gain knowledge from my students' perspective of what's going on in their world. And that's extraordinarily valuable to me, given my focus on them."

GREATEST SOCIAL TRAITS

Responsiveness. Loftin has built a strong reputation on social media for his timely responses to inquiries from students and other stakeholders. During my interview with the then-president of Texas A & M, he talked about how he would respond to between 25 and 30 requests daily via social media. There are few higher ed leaders on social media as committed to serving their students as Loftin, who responds to and acknowledges all manner of questions, from IT technical issues to policy decisions. Loftin also credits social media for helping him to better serve and remain accountable to his constituents whether he is on or off campus.

Delegation. Part of what makes Loftin's social media approach so effective is that rather than attempting to resolve every issue that comes his way, he instead focuses on delegating social-media-raised issues to his leadership and administrative teams. Due to the significant demands on Loftin's time, he could not effectively address every issue brought forward to him on social media while also fulfilling his daily duties as a higher ed senior leader. While Loftin personally responds to individuals who reach out to him via social media, he delegates certain matters to individuals more qualified to address them (e.g. he forwards facility issues to the facilities team; IT issues to the IT team). However, one thing that Loftin does not delegate is control of his social media accounts, which he manages day-to-day.

Consistency. Loftin regularly and consistently delivers content that his followers have come to welcome and expect. From photo updates of his travels on and off campus, to announcements of institutional achievements or initiatives, to the aforementioned responses to student inquiries, Loftin never lets more than a few hours or days pass without sharing content on one of his social media accounts. In part, it's Loftin's consistency that has helped his follower base grow, as users become accustomed to the kinds of content he shares and often return to his accounts to find similar content again and again.

Chapter 3

—

#GoneViral

Life moves pretty fast on social media, and higher ed leaders need to be aware of this before entering the space. News, both good and bad, along with rumors and innuendo, can spread quickly across a social network, and often the more salacious and scandalous the story, the more interest it garners.

College or university presidents need to understand how social media channels can amplify controversial stories. When social media users catch wind of a controversy, they have the opportunity not only to spread the story to their own personal networks and those of their followers, but also to comment on the story with their own views and feedback. Some senior leaders may not be used to the speed with which stories, both positive and negative, can go viral on social media.

In February 2014, Bryan College in Dayton, Tenn., faced a public relations issue that escalated quickly on social media (and eventually gained national media attention) when the Christian college's president and trustees altered its statement of belief to say that Adam and Eve were in fact historical figures. Within a matter of days, students, alumni, and faculty took to social media to air their displeasure with the decision. What emerged from those virtual discussions were tangible real-life actions affecting the college and its reputation. In the span of a few days, faculty voted "no confidence" in their president, with some leaving their positions in protest. Meanwhile, President Stephen Livesay, who is not active on social media, downplayed the seriousness of the issues at his institution to local reporters. Students used the speed of social networks like Twitter and Facebook to quickly organize on-campus protests in the weeks that followed and to have their voices heard by the college's administration.

Social media has undeniably become the platform of choice for 21st-century student activists and other institutional stakeholders looking to raise issues that are important to them. Higher ed leaders who wish to engage with these stakeholders need to recognize that social media channels are often the first spaces in which controversial matters relating to your institution are discussed and disseminated.

Many of the presidents I spoke to firmly believed that being well prepared for what to expect when beginning to use social media was a key component of succeeding within that world and advancing personal, professional, and institutional interests in the process. But how do you go about preparing yourself for the viral nature of social media?

In later chapters, you'll read about developing your personal social media strategy, including a risk management plan to guide your approach to handling controversy in the social media environment. But in this chapter we'll look how and why bad news travels so fast on social media, discuss the importance of crisis communications, and talk about what you can do to protect your own and your institutional reputations.

READILY ACCESSIBLE

Part of what makes social media such an exciting but also dangerous place for higher ed leaders is the fact that it is a democratized space in which users can instantaneously share information with a mass audience without going through any kind of filtering process. What's great about this is that your stakeholders can share (and you can access) immediate feedback on an initiative or activity in the blink of an eye and do so for free. This also provides you with the ability to break news about your institution to stakeholders before anyone else. What's challenging about this is that users can also share founded and unfounded comments and feedback about whatever's on their minds, and there's little anyone can do to stop that. Anyone who has the power to create a social media account also has the power to spread whatever information they see fit, whether or not it happens to be true. But not all bad news and rumors go viral, and you don't have to sit idly by as these issues spread across social media. Having your strategic advisers or communications team actively monitoring social media for certain keywords or issues relating to the Office of the President or the institution itself can empower you to proactively tackle troublesome topics that are starting to gain momentum on social media.

NO GATEKEEPERS

In the mainstream media world, stories or rumors that come forward are vetted for accuracy. If a rumor proves to be false, more often than not that can be sniffed out by media professionals seeking substantiation. In the social media landscape, unfounded rumors have legs based not on evidence but rather on how salacious the story might be. This lack of a gatekeeper responsible for fact-checking stories means that information that is partly or completely false can spread across social media, and you or your institution could be the only sources able to set the record straight.

The key in attempting to address rumors or spin on social media is to be strategic and consistent in your approach to responding. Assess whether the rumors are in fact spreading, or whether they are isolated to one rogue account or profile. If the unfounded or misinformation is starting to spread to multiple users, don't informally address the rumors without first investigating the situation. Gather as much information as you can about the story, separate fact from fiction, and work with your strategic advisers to develop your key messages in response. Stay consistent in those messages, address any follow-up questions that come up, and strive to be transparent about your process and sources of information. Many rumors and bad-news stories that spread on social media can be addressed by simply explaining the full story and combating innuendo with facts. Disseminate the facts using all the communications channels available to you and your team, including your personal and institutional social media accounts as well as your institution's website.

WORDS CARRY INFLUENCE

In February 2014, University of Iowa President Sally Mason made some controversial comments about campus sexual assaults—namely, that ending them would be an impossible task "given human nature"—that resulted in a social media firestorm. Activist groups across the United States pounced on the comments, mounting an aggressive social media campaign, regardless of the fact that Mason had been very proactive in addressing the issue at her institution, had an impressive track record of achievement, and herself had been a victim of assault in the 1970s.

In response to the activists' social media efforts, Mason, who does not have a presence on social media, and her team took to social, web-based, and mainstream channels to propose a six-point plan for addressing and responding to sexual assault on campus, acknowledging that her comments were hurtful and then changing the nature of the conversation to one about finding solutions to the problem rather than merely focusing on what she had said.

This situation demonstrates how social media has changed the game for college or university presidents. Mason's comments were not initially made on any social network, but the controversy spread like wildfire on social media. As previously mentioned, social media is now the platform of choice for student activists, and the only way Mason could tackle the issue was addressing it head-on and using all available communication tools, including social media. Had Mason been active on social media, could she have helped to ameliorate or address the issue on behalf of her institution? That remains unclear. But inevitably, her team decided that as part of its communications approach, the best way to reach stakeholders was through social media channels.

A PROACTIVE APPROACH

Higher ed leaders can adapt to the speed and amplification of social media by taking a proactive approach in how they respond to emerging issues or rumors on the verge of going viral. By having your strategic advisers actively and regularly monitor the discussions taking place on social media about you, your staff, students, faculty, and the institution as a whole, you can ensure that you are not caught off guard when or if these stories start to gain traction. Almost every social media platform enables users to perform keyword searches, and social media search engines like Topsy and Smashfuse enable searches for ongoing and backdated conversations about a particular subject area across a variety of networks. More established tools like Google Alerts, emailed directly to one's inbox, can also be helpful in tracking issues being discussed online. Outside of issues that a president wishes to monitor directly, the responsibility of actively monitoring social networks can be delegated to strategic advisers and communications staff who can provide regular reports to the president.

DEVELOP KEY MESSAGES

Actively monitoring developing issues will also enable you to work with your strategic advisers on preemptive key messages and crisis communications plans to address the issue and your institutional positioning on the subject. These messages don't have to be tailored to social media, but it is advisable to create two versions of key messages, those for mainstream media and those directly for social media, particularly social platforms with character limits like Twitter. Key messages should address issues directly and should bring clarity to a particular story, not further obfuscate matters. Crisis communications plans should include messages to use, on social media and elsewhere, in case the situation escalates in a negative direction. Higher ed leaders and strategic advisers should also develop social media FAQs about particular issues. Given the social media proclivity toward two-way engagement, stakeholders and observers may have follow-up questions about an issue, and leaders as well as institutions should be prepared to address those questions with transparent responses.

#YOUROWNCHOICE

Social media is a communications channel that doesn't always get stories right, but it does offer organizational senior leaders a platform through which to share the facts and do so quickly. This opportunity, to be recognized during challenging times as a trusted source of information to internal and external institutional stakeholders, is one of the reasons why higher ed leaders have taken so keenly to social media. We live in an era where higher ed stakeholders expect radical transparency from their institutional leaders, and the fast-paced nature of social media, while a double-edged sword in terms of spreading bad news quickly, is equally useful at spreading good news just as fast. The advantage that social-media-active presidents have over their non-social counterparts is that they can directly address issues in their own voice, using the speed of social media to respond with greater agility. After all, a higher ed leader on social media is always just one video or blog post, tweet, or update away from setting the record straight. Many of the presidents I spoke to appreciated that their social media profiles had become authoritative sources of information about their institutions, relied upon by a variety of stakeholders. The number of higher ed leaders who believe their social media presence is helping to more effectively and accurately tell their institution's stories is on the rise.

STRATEGIC ADVISER'S SHARE

- Work with your president to actively monitor issues relating to your institution being discussed on social media. Develop a list of keywords that you will regularly search for, or set up alerts to ensure you stay on top of the conversations tied to those words.

- Actively monitor isolated issues that are being discussed by stakeholders to identify those that could develop into more serious matters affecting institutional or presidential reputations.

- If an institutional issue appears to be gaining momentum, work with your president to develop and identify key messages and FAQs to address the issue and potential associated follow-up questions. Focus on being as transparent as possible, since your stakeholders will essentially be expecting as much. You also don't want to be caught off guard with certain questions, scrambling for messaging, or appearing to be avoiding answering certain questions.

PRESIDENT'S POST

- Recognize and understand the speed of social media before you pursue a personal profile on a social network. Good news and bad news travel fast on social media, so work with your team to actively monitor the key issues and search terms that are relevant to you and your institution. Social media will also amplify those issues, potentially making them damaging to personal, professional, and institutional reputations if not preemptively addressed.

• Understand that your social media followers and stakeholders will expect a high level of radical transparency from your social media account, so be prepared to address any issues facing you or your institution directly.

• You can prepare for this kind of engagement by working with your strategic advisers to develop key messages and a list of projected FAQs and corresponding responses to ensure you are ready for any inquiries that may come your way.

• Ensure your own or your institutional accounts are the official sources of news and information and that you control the news cycle. Proactively address issues by sharing information openly and taking the initiative to provide relevant details relating to an outstanding issue.

Chapter 4

—

#KnowYourOptions

Choosing a social media tool is a lot like buying a car: On the surface, your options appear endless, but once you start investigating makes, models, prices, and your needs, you quickly learn that not every car is right for you. In social media shopping, like in car shopping, once you consider all the relevant factors, you may be able to narrow down which social media platforms will best meet your needs.

Look closely at the social media channels and platforms available to you before deciding on the ones you may wish to commit to. Each channel brings with it a unique culture, style, conventions, and etiquette, and you should familiarize yourself with those norms before venturing onto those networks. Exploring which social media platforms other presidents are employing is also a good idea.

Most of the college and university presidents I spoke to as part of my research ventured into their first social media experiences fueled by personal and professional curiosity about these emerging technologies. The most common first social media tool employed by the presidents I interviewed was a blog, followed often by a Facebook or Twitter account. One interview participant recalled entering the social media world in 2004, before the launch of now-dominant platforms like Facebook and Twitter. While most of these presidents embraced social media without being prompted by their institutions, some newer presidents were advised by strategic advisers or communications and marketing staff to engage on social media as soon as possible after their hiring as a means of connecting with internal and external stakeholders.

The presidents I interviewed mentioned a variety of social media platforms and strategies that they have either employed themselves (see Fig. 4.1) or observed being employed by other higher ed leaders.

All 22 presidents I spoke to were active users of Twitter, but that simply reflects the fact that I used Twitter as a participant recruitment tool and is not necessarily reflective of Twitter's penetration rate among Canadian and American presidents.

The 11 participants from the United States all used Facebook to engage with key constituencies. This marked the biggest difference between Canadian and American respondents in their use of social media tools: Only five

Canadian participants used Facebook to personally engage with stakeholders in their role as president. The American participants were also far more aggressive than the Canadians in their use of emerging social media tools, including Instagram, Flipboard, Reddit, and Google+.

Use of both LinkedIn and YouTube was comparable among the two sets of interviewees. Three Americans and three Canadians used LinkedIn, but only one American and one Canadian indicated they used a presidential YouTube account.

Lastly, while three Canadian and four American presidents said they had used blogs, many added that they were not active users, or noted that although they had once actively managed a presidential blog, they were no longer regular users of the platform.

Fig. 4.1: Comparative chart of current social media tools used by Canadian and American interview participants from my 2013 research study.

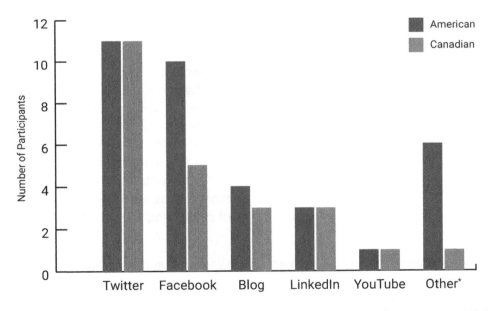

*Other channels included Instagram, Reddit, Flipboard, Google+, Yammer, and Flickr.

Research indicates that organizational leaders who are effective on social media often select their platforms very carefully and based, in part, on their skills and strengths. In a June 2013 article on Entrepreneur.com titled "The Social Media Rules for CEOs," Christopher Hann advised senior executives to choose the social media platform that plays to their strengths: "If you're the CEO of a small company with a modest budget for social media, choose the platform on which you're most likely to succeed. If you're pithy, you might do best with Twitter. If you're more comfortable in front of a camera, get yourself on YouTube."

So, which social networks might play to your strengths? Here is the list of the ones most commonly used by higher ed leaders and the skills they require.

BLOGGING

What it is

Blogging is among the more established social media approaches, one that most higher ed leaders are familiar with. A blog enables you to post long-form text-based or mixed-media content (e.g. text and images or videos). A blog can be housed either on your institutional website or on an external blogging service like Blogger or Blogspot. (Some argue that a blog appears more trustworthy and authoritative when hosted on a campus website, and others add that hosting a blog internally can protect a president's content from changes in terms of service on external social media platforms.)

How you can use it

Blogs give higher ed leaders the opportunity to expound on a subject in great breadth and depth and often offer the option for blog followers to comment on posts, with the expectation that comments will be responded to. Blogs often land high on search engine results because of relevant keywords tagged within them, making them a great tool through which to spread institutional news and have your voice as a higher ed leader heard in an unfiltered fashion. As both writer and editor of your blog, you decide what content to share through this channel and how exactly you wish to do so.

Who you'll reach

Typical audiences you'll reach through your blog include students, faculty, staff, alumni, government officials, and media.

Skills required

Effective blogging requires the blogger to be comfortable delivering long-form written content. This often suits the communications styles of many higher ed leaders, thanks to their familiarity with doing so outside of social media.

To make the most of the medium, bloggers need to take advantage of the platform's potential for prompting interactive discussion. Some college and university presidents struggle in embracing the two-way engagement element of a blog, either by not responding to reader comments or not offering open-forum comment functionality on their blogs at all. A key element of what makes a blog "social" is the potential for readers to comment, and for those comments to be addressed and responded to by the blogger.

Bloggers need to be aware of, and attentive to, what their stakeholders might actually want to read about. Those who do not may fail to offer compelling content that attracts blog readership beyond a small minority of institutional constituents.

Why a blog?

Choose this tool if you want an authoritative social media space through which to share your opinions, vision, achievements, and updates with your campus community.

FACEBOOK

What it is

The most popular social network in the world, Facebook is founded on the concept of sharing news, content (e.g. images, links and videos), and information with your community of friends. Not all content posted to Facebook is publicly accessible, but as with other social media tools, always assume content shared on Facebook is being made public.

How you can use it

The great appeal for college and university presidents is the opportunity to reach a wide range of institutional stakeholders through their Facebook posts. Higher ed leaders use Facebook in two primary ways: either personal accounts, in which they share a mix of institutional and non-institutional content limited to their network of Facebook friends (chosen by the presidential user), or public profiles that any Facebook user can access, through which they share primarily institutional content about themselves and their campus. Readers are likely to be interested in a mix of comments and updates about the institution, images from campus events, personal anecdotes, success stories and achievements, and other messages that align with the strategic priorities of the institution. Facebook users also expect college or university presidents to be accessible through their accounts to answer questions and address emerging or existing issues at their institutions.

Who you'll reach

Typical audiences you'll reach on Facebook include alumni, parents, current students, faculty, and staff.

Skills required

Higher ed leaders using Facebook must demonstrate an ability or willingness to share a range of personal and professional updates through their accounts, including text, image, and video-based content.

Facebook is predominantly a platform in which authentic, conversational, and somewhat informal engagement takes place between users, and so higher ed leaders should be prepared to adhere to the conventions of the platform in their own communications approach.

Why Facebook?

Choose this tool if you wish to engage in two-way dialogue with your most valued internal and external stakeholders and share updates with them about your institutional vision, personal life, and campus success stories.

TWITTER

What it is

The highly popular microblogging platform, known globally for its 140-character limit on its users' updates, has been widely adopted by individuals and brands alike. Twitter enables individuals to instantaneously share content—including text, images, and videos—through hyperlinks, and all content posted to Twitter is immediately publicly accessible.

How you can use it

Higher ed leaders have embraced Twitter as a channel through which they can directly engage with their institution's key internal and external stakeholders. Check out some of the presidential profiles in this book for examples of how higher ed leaders are using Twitter to achieve a variety of objectives and priorities.

Who you'll reach

Typical audiences you'll reach on Twitter include students (both current and prospective), faculty, staff, alumni, other college or university presidents, thought leaders, higher ed policy experts, media, government officials, donors, and partners.

Skills required

Twitter users expect consistent and compelling content from the accounts they follow, and the expectations on higher ed leaders are no different. College and university presidents must deliver meaningful and up-to-date institutional information to their followers and do so with regularity.

Twitter users are also expected to engage in two-way conversations with their followers, and so higher ed leaders wishing to establish a recognized presence on Twitter should be prepared to engage in frank and informal conversations as well. Individuals who are uncomfortable taking part in such informal and unscripted exchanges may have difficulty adapting to the conventions of Twitter.

Higher ed leaders who use Twitter need to be able to express themselves concisely, both piquing interest and getting a point across within tight limits. There's no room here for measured, well-developed arguments or a narrative style.

Why Twitter?

Choose this tool if you want to engage in quick and diverse conversations with a variety of internal and external stakeholders in a venue that is publicly accessible and can boost both your own profile and your institution's; and if, at the same time, you have embraced the risks associated with these conversations because you believe the potential benefit-return for your institution is greater than the potential costs.

YOUTUBE

What it is

The most popular video sharing website in the world, YouTube has become an online hub where brands and individuals alike have a level and democratized playing field for sharing and spreading their video content.

How you can use it

Higher ed leaders and their institutions have already taken to YouTube as a way to showcase institutional stories and celebrate achievements. In particular, college and university presidents have had success sharing video content on YouTube featuring themselves discussing institutional issues or announcements.

Who you'll reach

Typical audiences you'll reach on YouTube include students, faculty, staff, alumni, and any number of external stakeholders and non-stakeholders, if your content goes viral, since all content on YouTube is publicly accessible. However, if your video content has limited appeal, don't expect it to have an impact on institutional priorities or results.

Skills required

Producing effective and resonant video content on YouTube will require a higher ed leader to secure video production support from the institution's technical staff. This will ensure video quality and production values are high.

Videos should be short, compelling, and to the point. There is no ideal YouTube video length, but anywhere from one to two minutes is advised, depending on the nature of the message being delivered. A higher ed leader should seek support from strategic advisers or the communications team regarding developing content that will appeal to institutional stakeholders, and then work with those advisers to develop video content that delivers key messages but also encourages engagement.

A higher ed leader should be prepared to respond to comments and questions generated by viewers once the video has been posted.

Why YouTube?

Choose this tool if you have a visually compelling message to share or a brief announcement with a visual component to it (e.g. the opening of a new campus building), or if you have visual footage of yourself engaging in an on-campus activity that can enhance perceptions of your institution or yourself.

GOOGLE+

What it is

This emerging social network, owned by Google, has millions of users globally. Individuals, brands, and organizations use it to connect with one another through text-based conversation and image and video sharing as well as engagement through video chat.

How you can use it

Higher ed leaders are increasingly taking to Google+ as their social network of choice because of the flexibility it offers to engage with users through a variety of means (e.g. video chat, instant messaging), and also because Google+ profiles appear higher in search engine results than profiles on other social networks.

Who you'll reach

Typical audiences you'll reach on Google+ include students, faculty, staff, alumni, some media, and other higher ed leaders.

Skills required

As with engagement on Twitter and Facebook, conversations on Google+ take on a casual and informal tone. A higher ed leader must abide by those conventions to be effective.

Users are agile and ready to engage with followers while employing a variety of communications skills and approaches, including video chat "hangouts," image sharing, and written content.

Higher ed leaders who have embraced Google+ are often effective in their two-way engagement, not solely sharing content with followers but conversing with them as well.

Why Google+?

Choose this tool if you are looking for a social network where your content can be more easily found in Google search results and through which you can share text, images, and video content easily with a number of your internal and external stakeholders.

LINKEDIN

What it is

One of the most popular business and employment networking sites in the world, LinkedIn is an invitation-based social network in which the only way to follow someone's profile is to be invited or for that person to accept your invitation. The profiles of higher ed leaders on LinkedIn feature up-to-date career summaries as well as a comprehensive skills assessments and a listing of major credentials and career achievements.

How you can use it

Higher ed leaders have been using LinkedIn for years to help advance their own careers by building their network of contacts, and also to share thought leadership content and enhance institutional stakeholder relationships. Higher ed leaders using LinkedIn effectively regularly share compelling and relevant thought leadership content or celebrate the achievements of their institutions. They do so by sharing links to articles, media releases, and infographics relating to their areas of specialization or expertise.

Who you'll reach

Typical audiences you'll reach through LinkedIn include students, faculty, staff, other higher ed leaders, industry partners, donors, and alumni. Brands, organizations, and professional societies also have a presence on LinkedIn, where contacts, conversations, and ideas relating to various industries are exchanged.

Skills required

Two-way engagement is encouraged on LinkedIn, so higher ed leaders should comment often on articles and content shared by their followers.

Less conversational than other social networks, LinkedIn is known as a platform through which followers communicate with one another in a more professional manner than on other channels. Users should be prepared to communicate their thoughts, opinions, and ideas in formal and thoughtful ways.

Why LinkedIn?

Choose this tool if you are looking to build your professional network and develop relationships with internal and external stakeholders that could enhance perceptions and advance priorities of your institution.

INSTAGRAM

What it is

This emerging image- and video-sharing social platform, widely popular among key demographic groups relevant to higher ed institutions, enables you to post images and videos from your day-to-day life, with the option of editing the photos you've uploaded using color filters. The social platform also offers you the flexibility to tag your photos and videos with relevant hashtags, making the content easier to search for and describing what's happening in them. Images and videos are then shared with your followers, who can view and "like" your uploaded content.

How you can use it

Higher ed leaders are using Instagram to document events they attend on and off campus and to share interesting sights and happenings that they experience in the course of their day. College and university presidents will often share photos from their travels, vacations, or unique visual spectacles at conferences or other events.

Who you'll reach

Typical audiences you'll reach with Instagram include students, faculty, staff, and alumni.

Skills required

Higher ed leaders using Instagram demonstrate a desire to share goings-on from their lives through images and videos.

The images, videos, content descriptions, and hashtags used on Instagram are all delivered in an informal conversational style that is both lighthearted and playful. Users need to be able to select and present visual content that is compelling, stimulating, current, and consistent.

Higher ed leaders on Instagram tend to be natural shutterbugs or even passionate photographers who believe in image sharing as a means of social media engagement.

Why Instagram?

Choose this tool if you're looking to share a lighter side of yourself by offering followers visual glimpses into your day-to-day experiences as a college or university president while also engaging with other users about the visual content they're sharing.

PINTEREST

What it is

In this globally popular image-based social network, users upload, share, and comment on visual content that is sorted by keywords and categories. Pinterest users who see visual content they find interesting can "pin" that content onto their personal Pinterest board as a means of expressing their areas of interest and passions.

How you can use it

Few if any higher ed leaders are active on Pinterest, but many of their institutions have accounts for sharing images of college events, student art work or research, and other visually compelling photo content.

Who you'll reach

Typical audiences you'll reach on Pinterest include students, faculty, staff, alumni, and other diverse external audiences.

Skills required

Users demonstrate a willingness to find and share compelling and dynamic visual content that reflects their areas of interest and that they think other Pinterest users will find either helpful or interesting.

College and university presidents who engage on Pinterest should have access to, and familiarity with, a sizable pool of campus-generated images that tell the institution's story or otherwise relate to their interests.

Why Pinterest?

Choose this tool if you believe the most effective way to tell your institution's story is through images; if you also believe the image content you have to share is both interesting and diverse; and if you have the desire to share that content regularly.

REDDIT

What it is

Reddit is a completely democratized platform with few if any limitations on appropriate language or content shared. In this globally recognized social network, users can "up-vote" or "down-vote" as well as comment on content—including images, videos, articles, and memes—that is shared by other users. Users come to Reddit to experience unfiltered information for which they will then assess newsworthiness. The component of primary interest to higher ed leaders is its Ask Me Anything (AMA) feature, in which Reddit users are able to ask questions of celebrities, professional athletes, or other individuals with high-profile positions who answer user-submitted questions in an unfiltered and direct fashion.

How you can use it

While neither Reddit nor its AMA feature are tools a college or university president can regularly employ for social media engagement, they can be used for special occasions in which a higher ed leader is looking to generate exposure for the institution, has compelling content to share, and recognizes and is prepared for the possibility that Reddit users may ask questions of a sensitive, personal, or inappropriate nature. More and more brands and public figures have increasingly embraced these risks because Reddit is so widely visited by diverse audiences around the globe. Content that has gone viral on Reddit will often filter its way to mainstream media days later.

Who you'll reach

Typical audiences you'll reach on Reddit include students, alumni, and media.

Skills required

Higher ed leaders using Reddit should be prepared for users to be fickle and particular about the content they like and dislike. Work with strategic advisers and communications staff to ensure content shared on Reddit is compelling, timely, and unique and offers a wide range of users a clear benefit-return for their investment of time.

In particular, a president wishing to partake in a Reddit AMA should be thoroughly prepared. AMA participants are looking for an insider's perspective on your life and work. Ensure that you and your strategic advisers have developed, in advance, key messaging you wish to deliver through your AMA session.

Why Reddit?

Choose this tool if you have compelling visual or text-based content to share that you think a mass audience would find intriguing. Alternately, choose this tool if you wish to partake in an Ask Me Anything session, in which you are prepared to answer deeply revealing questions, because you believe you can offer intriguing insights about yourself, your institution, and your profession to Reddit audiences.

TUMBLR

What it is

This emerging microblogging platform is something like Twitter—without the character limits, but with a similar emphasis on minimalism and instantaneous access. It enables individuals, brands, and organizations to easily create blogs called Tumblrs, through which they can seamlessly integrate image, text, and video content for their followers (see Fig. 4.2).

How you can use it

Tumblrs enable higher ed leaders to offer their followers compelling, timely, and regular content that is visually stimulating and takes on a light and conversational tone.

Who you'll reach

Typical audiences you'll reach on Tumblr include students, staff, faculty, alumni, media, and other external stakeholders who may be users of this

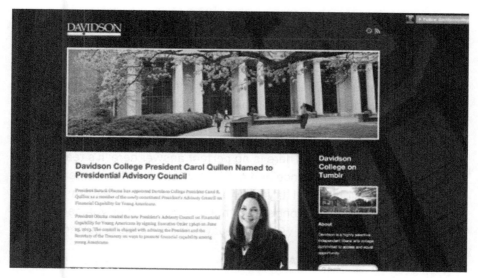

Fig. 4.2: A screen shot of the Tumblr for Davidson College (located in Davidson, N.C.), featuring an update about its president, Carol Quillen.

social network or who are searching for relevant keywords tied to your Tumblr post.

Skills required

College or university presidents who are successful on Tumblr demonstrate a casual and informal communications style that when mixed with compelling visual stories can help to humanize them and make them appear more accessible to key stakeholders.

Those looking to use Tumblr must be committed to making regular updates. They should work with strategic advisers and communications staff to develop a content-sharing calendar to ensure their accounts are not left unattended for long periods of time, and that updates align with institutional interests.

Why Tumblr?

Choose this tool if you want to share dynamic text, image, or video content in a blog-style format but are not looking to generate a great deal of narrative, and if you wish to engage with a diverse and emerging social media community who will actively share and respond to your content (if they find it compelling).

#YOUROWNCHOICE

Higher ed leaders who choose a social media platform where they are asked to communicate in a way that doesn't make them feel comfortable or that doesn't align with their skill set, communications style, or interests are likely setting themselves up for failure on that social network. Whichever social network you choose to engage on, you should conduct research about that platform and decide for yourself whether that's the car you want to drive off into the sunset. There is no perfect answer here; it's really just a matter of personal preference and experimentation. At the same time, no social media decision is final. If you try a particular social platform but, after a certain period of time, no longer feel that it works for you, you can always delete that account. I wish it were that easy when it came to buying cars.

STRATEGIC ADVISER'S SHARE

• Work with your president to research which social media platforms may or may not align with his skills and interests.

• Encourage your president to experiment with certain networks to see which ones might work for her. She can consider doing this experimentation anonymously or as herself, whichever she is comfortable with.

• If your president chooses to stop using a particular social network, be sure to delete the account after he has officially decided to move on.

• Once your president has chosen a particular network, provide support by reminding her of the conventions and norms on that social media channel, and work with her to develop content that is in line with those norms.

PRESIDENT'S POST

• Research your social media options and identify which platforms may or may not work for you. Are you comfortable with the conventions and communications style on the social network in question? Do you feel you can advance personal, professional, and institutional interests using this social network?

• Work with your strategic advisers to identify potential networks that might work for you. Start investigating the social networks used by your counterparts at other campuses. What elements of their engagement approach do you like and dislike? Which strategies could you employ in your social media engagement?

• Experiment with social networks that interest you, either anonymously or as yourself, but remember to delete those accounts you choose to abandon.

SOCIAL PROFILE: @HJTTHOMPSON

Dr. Tom Thompson, President, Olds College

BIO IN BRIEF

- Has served as president of Olds College in Olds, Alberta, since 2001
- Served as president of Grande Prairie Regional College in Grande Prairie, Alberta, from 1997 to 2001
- Obtained his Ed.D. in higher education administration, with a governance research focus, at the University of Calgary in 2008
- Led Olds College in launching a capital campaign that has already garnered significant support to transform the college and enhance learning opportunities in Olds, Calgary, and Alberta
- Currently active on Twitter, LinkedIn, blog

Source: "Thompson on Governance" blog (http://blog.thompsonongovernance.com/biography)

SOCIAL QUOTES

On jumping in to social media: "A president inhabits a position that is a fairly lonely place and you don't normally have a tendency to reach out, and as a result, I think, a president would have to overcome feelings of apprehension before jumping in to social media. They would have to overcome feelings of not wanting to appear out of step or not with it ... A president has to be willing to ask for help from those who are competent in social media."

On the dangers of misinterpreted conversations: "You do have people on [social media] who are watching and reading and are forming opinions and from time to time will interpret or misinterpret well-targeted relationship developments particularly with political masters as being … unsavory … And in turn, you could suffer backlash on the very instrument that you're using to nurture and grow political relationships."

GREATEST SOCIAL TRAITS

Relationship development. One of Thompson's great strengths in terms of his social media engagement has been his ability to foster and develop strategic relationships with key stakeholders that can help him to advance his institution's interests. From government officials and media to students, faculty, and other higher ed leaders, Thompson shares content as many social-media-active presidents do, but also has a clear focus on engaging in conversations that can help Olds College to achieve its strategic objectives and priorities. In my interview with Thompson, he told me how relationships he had developed on social media had helped him to arrange face-to-face meetings with key stakeholders that eventually led to increased support for his institution. In part, Thompson is able to develop such relationships by identifying which key stakeholders are active on social media, consistently engaging with those stakeholders, and discussing matters and issues of mutual interest.

Relationship management. Once Thompson has developed strategic relationships on social media, he does a masterful job of managing those relationships and ensuring they remain active. Thompson regularly communicates with those stakeholders with whom he maintains strategic relationships, offering them information about his institution's successes, key initiatives, and future plans, while also diversifying content to ensure the conversation is not solely one-dimensional or one-way. Part of what makes Thompson's relationship management approach so effective is that he does not go long periods of time without engaging with key stakeholders, and he takes the initiative in reaching out to them.

Strategic messaging. The other element of Thompson's social media approach that is so effective is his consistent delivery of strategic messaging that aligns with the priorities of his institution. While he includes personal updates and shares pictures from events he is attending, he mostly focuses on messaging that supports the major initiatives and plans of his institution. As mentioned, Thompson's social media updates are not solely limited to strategically aligned content, but it does make up a majority of what he shares. In particular, this strategic content is offered to key external stakeholders, including government officials, partners, and donors.

Chapter 5

—

#NoRightWay

There is more than one way to bake a cake, dive into a pool, or make a bed. There is also certainly more than one way for a higher ed leader to approach engaging on social media. Yet another recommendation emanating from my research is that there is not one social media approach, channel, or strategy that universally applies to every college or university president.

Your social media approach is personal to you, and as I've advised, you should not attempt to behave on a social network in a way that is outside your comfort zone. That is to say, content you share through social networks should never fall outside the realm of something you might share in your face-to-face contact with key stakeholders. If you feel uncomfortable sharing personal information or chiming in on controversial topics, you are under no obligation to do so, but you should be very careful when you do. As we discussed in Chapter 3, social media can be a volatile space where bad news travels fast and can turn into a more serious issue.

Effectively communicating on social media is not the result of embracing one communications philosophy over another. However, a key finding from my research was the importance for higher ed leaders to present versions of their professional and personal identities that reflect well on themselves and their institutions.

There are no clear techniques for college and university presidents to employ in their social media engagement that can guarantee the achievement or advancement of a particular result or objective. However, while researchers in industry and academia have not established a conclusive set of actions a senior leader can take to achieve success on social media, some believe a specific type of leader possessing certain traits is most likely to succeed.

One key trait is strong communications skills. Whether alone or with the assistance of strategic advisers, including professional communicators, senior leaders with strong communications skills often deliver messaging through social media that is clear, authentic, and persuasive.

THREE MODELS FOR CONTENT CREATION

While there may not be a right or wrong way to use social media, there are some approaches that the presidents I spoke to believe are more effective than others. In preparation for writing this book, I spent months observing the social media activity of hundreds of higher ed leaders from Canada and the United States. Through those observations and my interviews, I identified several social media content generation models being employed by Canadian and American college and university presidents. These models represent the different ways in which presidential social media accounts are currently being managed across a variety of social networks, including Facebook, Twitter, and LinkedIn. These content generation models can be divided into three main types.

The ghostwriter model

This model refers to presidents whose social media accounts are run by their own office's staff or their communications and marketing teams and are either ambiguous or explicit about the fact that the president is not supplying the actual content. The presidents interviewed overwhelmingly argued that this model was not particularly effective, given the expectations of transparency and authenticity within the social media context.

One American university president pointed out that he could handle the responsibility of his own social media account and wanted to maintain control over his social media presence: "Having someone else do an account in somebody's name, posing as that person, [is] disingenuous … I would have a fear of somebody making a misstep in my name. If I do my own misstep, that's on me. But if somebody else does that … I wouldn't feel like I have control of that situation." A growing body of research supports the viewpoint held by interviewees that the ghostwriter model is not an effective use of social media as a means of advancing organizational or personal interests. Institutional stakeholders want to connect with people and not ambiguous entities via social media, and this approach does not allow for person-to-person contact.

The hybrid model

This model refers to social media accounts under the name of a particular institutional president or the Office of the President where content is generated jointly by the president and institutional staff. Often, the president signs or initials personal communications to indicate when a post or tweet is coming directly from the president and not the staff.

In a similar division of labor that also falls under the hybrid approach, many of the higher ed leaders I spoke to highlighted their use of administrative staff in assisting them with their social media engagement, without actually writing on their behalf. Rather, these leaders indicated that staff would support them by handling referrals across the institutional community.

For example, University of Missouri Chancellor R. Bowen Loftin, whom I interviewed while he was president of Texas A & M, described receiving Facebook messages or tweets 25 to 30 times per day and either responding to each inquiry or delegating the request to someone in his administration. Loftin doesn't ask his staff or strategic advisers to communicate on his behalf through his social media accounts, but rather uses them to help him find the answers to the inquiries he receives from students. Loftin also expressed a sincere desire to respond daily to student inquiries.

The hybrid model encourages the delegation of some social media responsibilities to people with the appropriate skills to communicate effectively through these channels; what it doesn't suggest is that these responsibilities be handed over completely to institutional staff.

The independent model

This model of content generation was the approach espoused by most higher ed leaders I spoke to throughout my research, and it is also the model most often recommended to senior leaders by social media researchers and consultants. There are new and increasing expectations on presidents to not only be effective leaders and decision-makers, but also to become authentic, radically transparent, and strategic communicators who embrace social media tools that can help them to tell their own and their institution's stories. Several of the presidents I interviewed went as far as to say that no other social media model could be nearly as effective as the independent approach. One American college president stated, "If you're out there to put out the voice of the president, in an officious sense, I don't think too many people are going to be interested. But if you are indeed yourself and they see the blend of the personal and professional, that is sort of how we all live these days, and I think that is far more likely to be successful."

To me, University of Cincinnati President Santa Ono best exemplifies the independent model. His social media presence showcases his institution in a positive light while also presenting him as an outgoing, friendly, accessible, and transparent leader. His day-to-day efforts to engage with internal and external stakeholders while celebrating his university's success stories and revealing elements of his personality and interests is both authentic and refreshing.

While content in the independent model may be generated by the presidents themselves, it is important to note that some presidents mentioned that they do not always formulate their thoughts, observations, and posts in isolation. St. Francis Xavier University President Kent MacDonald, whom I interviewed while he was president of Algonquin College, revealed that he did not have a writer or public relations strategist providing him with content to share on his social media channels, but he did mention using communications staff for advice on whether to discuss certain sensitive issues on those platforms. Other research also supports the notion of trusted advisers, such as communications staff, providing counsel to senior leaders on the general tone and approach of their social media engagement because of their familiarity with two-way communication. Furthermore, the independent model is often perceived to be a more authentic communication approach, a strategy some researchers consider a linchpin of effective leadership in the 21st century.

FIVE STYLES OF PRESIDENTIAL PRESENCE

My research on higher ed leaders and their engagement on social media also explored how college and university presidents were using their accounts in different ways and for different purposes. Again, none of the approaches were either right or wrong; they were simply different, and reflected the personal preferences of each higher ed leader. I identified five distinct types of social media approaches being employed by higher ed leaders. These observations, while not necessarily reflective of all types of engagement by college and university presidents across all social networks, provide an understanding of how certain presidents manage their online presence differently from others. In particular, these different types of social media approaches showcase the variety of content presidents are sharing with stakeholders through their accounts.

The customer servant

This is a higher ed leader who uses social media to respond to all manner of questions and queries from potential and current students, faculty, and staff. From IT issues to difficulties with admission, these presidents take a hands-on approach to customer service, and it can be said they are setting the tone for their institutions with respect to customer service. Paul LeBlanc, president of Southern New Hampshire University, explained that his social media approach has helped him to establish a reputation on campus for getting things done and helping students with their problems, both large and small.

In this Twitter exchange, we see LeBlanc in action, serving one of his customers:

@andynieves: @snhuprez @SNHU mySNHU isn't working and I am trying to finalize my class registration for tomorrow. HELP?

> **@snhuprez:** @andynieves @SNHU Wish I could. But will let IT know as they are the experts.

The institutional promoter

This is a college or university president who uses social media to share content about the institution and not much else. These higher ed leaders are focused solely on using social media channels to boost institutional interests and do not share personal content. For example, Webster University President Elizabeth Stroble explained she uses Twitter in this way to celebrate the successes and achievements of her university: "Twitter suits my style of communication and community building quite well … I pick pieces and parts of stories about our people, our places, and I spread them out for other members of our community to know." Many higher ed leaders toot their own or their institution's horns on social media, and this can help build awareness about their institutions.

In the example below, Dillard University President Walter Kimbrough does this effectively through one of his tweets:

@hiphopprez: Just had a fantastic meeting with KIPP [Knowledge is Power Program]. Dillard will soon be announced as the newest partner school—the 3rd HBCU to become a partner.

The socially inconsistent president

These are presidents who maintain social media accounts but do not actively use them. The impact of these accounts is questionable in that they occupy space on a particular social network, but they may not project an image of the president or the institution that is particularly desirable or engaging. One Canadian college president revealed that it is undeniably challenging to maintain an active and consistent social media presence while balancing numerous demands from across the campus community: "It's hard to keep up with it all the time … some say the rules are that you should post something daily or twice a day, and given my schedule, that's not always possible … There are times where I'll go dry on it, but there are other times where I'm more active." No higher ed leader can be active on social media at all times, but they should avoid long periods of time where they do not engage with followers.

In the example below, Rice University President David Leebron goes almost a month between tweets:

@**davidleebron** [May 31]: Tough end to tough game as Owls lose 3–2 in 11th inning. Tomorrow is a new day.

@**davidleebron** [Jun 25]: Exactly 10 yrs ago, I moved to Houston w/ my family, & only vague sense of what lay ahead. Thank you Rice & Houston for a wonderful decade!

The oversharing non-strategist

These are higher ed presidents using social media for, at times, unclear objectives. Their content and engagement is a mixture of personal and professional conversations with students, staff, and counterparts, with topics ranging from their institutions to popular memes. At times, these individuals might reveal too much personal content and be inconsistent in their sharing of institutional content and key messages, reflecting on their institution in an undesirable way. While few of the presidents I interviewed demonstrated the outright qualities of an oversharing non-strategist through their social media profiles, many noted that effective social media engagement required a more strategic approach. One American university president pointed out that he tends to be very selective about the content he shares via social media and evaluates whether that content helps to advance his institution's strategic interests or harms his own personal reputation: "I'll often ask myself or remind myself, is this something I want our constituents to know about me, or anyone else that I'm talking about, or conversing with, or posting pictures of on Facebook and Twitter."

In the examples below, former Crown College President Rick Mann tweets on a variety of different subjects, but how are they linked, and how do they advance his college's strategic priorities or objectives?

@**presidentmann:** On a flight with the Seattle Storm WNBA team. Certainly a tall group of women! They weren't too happy about losing to MN last night.

@**presidentmann**: Congrats to Crown soccer player Megan Wright, UMAC Player of the Week and leading UMAC in goals and points … . http://ow.ly/dZMSd

> **@presidentmann:** Congrats to freshman Crown golfer Reed Sorensen, UMAC Golfer of the Week. http://ow.ly/dZMzE

> **@presidentmann:** TIME: How different generations of Americans try to find work. http://ow.ly/dXOlc

> **@presidentmann:** People leaving California for Texas. http://ow.ly/dXOtF

> **@presidentmann:** Minnesota Road Trip: Kayak Lake Superior, Bike/Hike Gooseberry Falls, Enjoy the fall colors. Priceless! http://ow.ly/i/XAxy

The socially active strategist

This type of higher ed leader approaches social media engagement with a strategy in mind. These leaders are often institutionally focused while mixing in some details about their personal lives. They engage in meaningful discussions with key stakeholder groups but also actively listen for issues being raised by key constituencies and relevant conversations with existing or potential influencers. Additionally, these users are constantly evaluating the effectiveness of their social media engagement with respect to advancing their own personal and professional interests as well as those of the institution. One American college president stated that he tried to align his social media activities with institutional strategies as often as possible when using these tools; he also endeavored to be consistent in his messages, his tone, and the regularity with which he posted to his accounts: "Social media to me is part of our retention strategy and part of our ... strategy for helping students to feel that they're part of the college and that somebody cares about them ... It's not as important that they know me ... But if by social media, I can help to indicate that I care from my role, as an individual that can, certainly, help some students to feel engaged."

Some of the presidents already mentioned in this book fall under the category of socially active strategists, including Santa Ono and R. Bowen Loftin. These examples of tweets directed to these leaders highlight their successful engagement approaches:

> **jason buken @ucskippy:** @PrezOno thanks for the love as u are the best president for #uc and its #students #faculty and #staff #oneteam.

> **@mizzoualumni:** Big thanks to @bowtieger for meeting our Governing Board today! Phenomenal champion for #Mizzou students and alumni.

#YOUROWNCHOICE

Whichever approach you choose to embrace as a higher ed leader on social media, it's important to reiterate that there is no black-and-white right or wrong answers here, only shades of gray. Your social media approach, much like your decision to engage on social media in the first place, must be a personal choice. How you engage should align with your communications style, it should fit into your busy schedule, and it should tap into the resources available to you as a college or university president. Your approach may be different from that of your competitor or counterpart, but that doesn't mean it's better or worse. When it comes to how you approach social media, there is no best practice—or rather, the best practice is the one that works for you.

STRATEGIC ADVISER'S SHARE

- Work with your president to identify which social media approach may be best suited to her communication style, schedule, and interests.

- Reiterate that there is no perfect approach to embrace or set of ground rules to implement. A president's social media approach must work for him.

- Ask your president how she wants to go about engaging on social media. Would she like to craft her own content? How can you work with her to support her social media engagement efforts?

PRESIDENT'S POST

- Recognize that there is no right or wrong way to approach your social media engagement.

- However, whichever approach you do embrace, align with your communications style, schedule, and interests. Also note that you and your counterparts may have different approaches to social media engagement, and that's fine.

- There is no reason why you cannot change your social media approach as you go. Experiment with approaches that you think might work for you, and assess what does and doesn't. What do your followers and stakeholders on social media respond to most? What content do they find most compelling? Use these findings to help steer you in the right direction with respect to how you approach your social media engagement.

Chapter 6

—

#YourSocialMediaRoleModel

There's no need to reinvent the wheel when it comes to how you choose to engage on social media. The online world is full of examples, and you can choose who you want to emulate. Your model could be one person, or it could be several. It might or might not be another higher ed leader. The choice of your role model, like so many other choices, is personal to you.

The social media activity of role models can help organizational senior leaders develop engagement practices that they believe might be suitable for them. While selecting role models and identifying their successful practices is no guarantee of success on social media, it can provide a starting point for senior leaders launching their presence on certain social networks. These role model accounts can help a president to see the potential opportunities and risks that exist when venturing into the social media sphere.

Searching for a social media role model, among your peers and beyond, will not only help you to learn the conventions of a particular social network, but it could also help you to understand what content you might consider sharing, how you might wish to engage with stakeholders and followers, and which social platforms may or may not work for you. I, along with many of the presidents I spoke with, would advise that before you venture into the space, find someone on social media who engages with stakeholders and shares content in a way that you consider particularly effective. While it isn't recommended that you mimic that role model exactly, identify the key strategies that social media personality is employing effectively and attempt to apply those practices to your own personal engagement.

CONSIDER DIFFERENT APPROACHES

As you evaluate potential role models, you need to look at the strategies and tactics each individual employs and whether that approach would suit your own communication style, personality, and interests.

For example, in the tweet below, University of Missouri Chancellor R. Bowen Loftin uses his account to take a stand on the issue of arts education funding in Missouri public schools:

> **@bowtieger:** MU produces powerful art educators that our public schools NEED! #savemizzouarted #muartedmatters

This might very well be the type of content you wish to share on your social media profile. Or you might see it as too contentious; if so, you would not select a role model who takes public stands on issues in the way Loftin does.

By contrast, in the tweet below, we see Dillard University President Walter Kimbrough sharing his passion and excitement about the NBA finals through his social media account:

> **@HipHopPrez:** Love the #NBAFinals press conferences. Definitely love watching LeBron mature & how he handles the questions.

Veering off into your personal interests might not be an approach you wish to employ on your presidential social media profile; then again, maybe sharing the activities you pursue outside your official role is something you could see yourself doing.

In both cases, there is no right or wrong answer. Only you can decide how you wish to approach your social media engagement as a higher ed leader.

ASSESS STRENGTHS

It is also important for higher ed leaders, with help from their strategic advisers, to evaluate what strengths they perceive their role models bring to the table. Some, like President Santa Ono of the University of Cincinnati, actively and consistently engage with students and alumni in lively banter that boosts institutional school spirit. Some do a great job of celebrating institutional donations and support, as in the tweet below from Bethany College President Scott Miller:

> **@BethanyCollege1:** Thanks! To the Bethany College Class of 1961 for the class gift of $136,660 presented at the Alumni Luncheon today …

Investigate what your role models do well and which of those traits you might be able to implement in your own social media approach and engagement. If you are unable to identify any discernible strengths in the social media approach of a potential role model, then that example might not be able to help you identify which strategies you might wish to employ.

IDENTIFY WEAKNESSES

Simultaneously, as you observe your potential role model's strengths, take a look at his or her weaknesses—at least, the weaknesses as you perceive them. The role model in question might see those same attributes as great strengths. As mentioned, it's all relative. Perhaps you think the individual in question shares too many personal details or engages in too many heated, negative, or inflammatory exchanges with followers and stakeholders. You might see the person's communication as not sufficiently focused on institutional stories, or too focused on news and happenings related to their campus. Identify these perceived weaknesses and make note of them for future reference. This will help inform your own rules of engagement (see Chapter 7) as well as your own social media strategy (see Chapter 9).

EVALUATE AGENDAS

As you review your social media role model candidates, ask yourself what their agenda might be and whether their approach and strategy could support objectives similar to your own. Does the role model in question appear to be engaging and developing relationships with key stakeholders? Is he solely focused on interacting with students and staff, or does he have an external focus? Does she attempt to boost school spirit and morale through the content she shares on social media, or is she more interested in creating and sharing thought leadership content? Perhaps his priorities and objectives are mixed or unclear and he doesn't have a specific agenda in terms of his social media engagement.

In the Twitter post below, President Paul LeBlanc of Southern New Hampshire University shares a picture of a custom graduation cake created by a parent of one his graduating students:

> **@snhuprez:** Love this graduation cake an SNHU mom made for her graduate this weekend: pic.twitter.com/9jk00jUh

Does this message support his strategic agenda with respect to what he is hoping to achieve through his social media activities? It very well might, if LeBlanc has placed a priority on boosting institutional pride and morale.

Whatever the agenda or objectives of the role models in question, the most important takeaway from assessing what they're trying to accomplish is whether their priorities might align with your own personal, professional, or institutional priorities. If they don't, seek out role models whose agenda appears to be more closely aligned with your own. If their plans appear to be in sync with yours, then they could be worth paying close attention to.

#YOUROWNCHOICE

No social media role model is perfect, and there may be only a select group of individuals whose approaches you truly admire. Still, conducting this environmental scan of comparable social media profiles will help to inform the kind of social media leader you wish to become. Learning from other leaders' strengths and weaknesses will also mean that your onboarding process will be quicker, and you may be able to avoid certain pitfalls that others have run into. Consider your search for social media role models a kind of rite of passage: Once you study the masters, you're all set to build on the shoulders of giants.

STRATEGIC ADVISER'S SHARE

- Work with your president to identify potential social media role models who exhibit strengths, qualities, and agendas that align with the communication style, skill set, and interests of your president.

- Start out with a list of fellow higher ed leaders on social media, but feel free to expand the list beyond that, if preferred.

- Pare down the list as needed based on the weaknesses your president identifies in each model's social media approach. Take note of those perceived weaknesses, and use them when developing your president's social media rules of engagement and strategy.

PRESIDENT'S POST

- In association with your strategic advisers, identify potential social media role models from your fellow higher ed leaders and beyond. Ask yourself, what is it about their social media approach and engagement that appeals to you? What do you think they do well? What are their areas of weakness? What are they trying to achieve through their social media activities?

- Take note of the elements of their social media approach that you like and dislike. Use this to inform your own social media approach and engagement style.

- Remember not to mimic exactly the style of your social media role models; find a way to take elements of their approach and apply it to your own. Create a style that is as unique as you are.

SOCIAL PROFILE: @HIPHOPPREZ

Dr. Walter Kimbrough, President, Dillard University

BIO IN BRIEF

- Became the seventh president of Dillard University in New Orleans, La., in 2012
- Served as president of Philander Smith College in Little Rock, Ark., from 2004 to 2012
- Earned degrees from the University of Georgia and Miami University in Ohio, as well as a doctorate in higher education from Georgia State University
- In 2010, named to the Ebony "Power 100" list of the doers and influencers in the African American community and cited by BachelorsDegree.com as one of 25 college presidents you should follow on Twitter
- Currently active on Twitter, Facebook, Google+, Instagram, LinkedIn, blog

Source: Dillard University website (http://www.dillard.edu/index. php?option=com_content&view=article&id=1053&Itemid=873)

SOCIAL QUOTES

On managing your own account: "I think it should be authentic ... There are accounts for presidents for Facebook and Twitter that they don't manage. That's counter to what social media is all about. If they're not going to be engaged, don't do it. It just makes those of us who do it stand out even more ... It has to be their choice, it has to be something they're comfortable with."

On being strategic: "For most presidents, it's about talking about how I want to use social media, how can I be strategic in my usage ... how do we use this as an advancement tool, how does this advance the institution, broaden our exposure, reach our influencers, those we want to influence, potential students, parents."

On celebrating your achievements: "I follow a good number of presidents ... I'm watching how they use it ... Talking about stories that they think students or their alums should read, stories about their institution, events on campus ... they use it as a promotional tool. Some ... will engage in more personal conversations ... It's personality-driven, and a common theme is presidents realizing that this is a way to toot our horns about what's happening on our campuses, and even if we do it just for that ... to me, it's worth it ... It's a free way to pat people and the institution on the back."

GREATEST SOCIAL TRAITS

Authentic engagement. One of Kimbrough's great differentiators in terms of his social media engagement approach is that the content he shares accurately and authentically reflects his diverse areas of interest. Much like other social-media-active higher ed leaders, Kimbrough offers his fair share of news, updates, and events relating to Dillard University, but he also delivers thought leadership content, views on a variety of local and national issues, and input on matters relevant to his role as a leader in the African American community, as well as other topics reflective of goings-on in his home base of New Orleans. Kimbrough believes a key to his success and recognition on social media has been his willingness to let students, faculty, staff, and other stakeholders get to know what he is all about as an individual through his social media presence.

Thought leadership. Kimbrough is also recognized for sharing input, ideas, and links on a variety of issues relevant to his role as president of Dillard University as well as matters for which he is considered a thought leader. From subjects close to his area of expertise—leadership and fundraising for historically black colleges and universities—to unemployment and the economy, Kimbrough offers content that is compelling, current, and reflective of his position as a leader on matters both higher-education-related and not. Kimbrough is able to share his thought leadership content with internal and external stakeholders instantaneously through social media, and the content he offers strengthens perceptions of him as a leader along with the institution he leads.

Celebrating institutional achievements. Kimbrough's social media accounts do an excellent job of highlighting his institutional success stories, and those stories are often complemented by images, videos, and articles about those achievements. Whether he is retweeting messages from faculty members or students on his Twitter account or sharing images from graduation ceremonies or fundraising events via Instagram, Kimbrough is a recognized institutional promoter whose social media approach blends Dillard-related content with a diverse mix of offerings for a number of different audiences. Kimbrough's social media accounts are also particularly effective when it comes to finding and reaching out to local media contacts with whom he can share news of his institution.

You're On

Chapter 7

—

#YourRulesOfEngagement

Some like it hot. Others do not.

Some higher ed leaders share personal content on social media, and others do not. Some presidents will not address controversial stories, while others will respond to them directly. Some will not add students or staff as social media followers or friends, and others will actively invite them to engage and communicate. According to my research, presidents should develop their personal rules of engagement for their social media interactions, seeking input, where appropriate, from strategic advisers, communications staff, and other social-media-active counterparts. It is important to note that, as with other decisions related to social media, your rules of engagement are personal to you and may not necessarily reflect views held by others.

This chapter outlines some areas of consideration for higher ed leaders with respect to developing their social media rules of engagement. While not comprehensive, the list that follows covers some of the decisions that the presidents I interviewed grappled with as they developed their own rules for operating in the social media space.

ADDRESSING CONTENTIOUS ISSUES

The presidents I interviewed had diverse views about using social media to discuss contentious issues tied to their institutions. In particular, there were those who believed social media was not the platform for controversial debates; they cited Twitter as an example of a network not necessarily suited to resolving such issues due to its restrictive character limits and free-for-all nature. However, a number of the presidents I observed through my research use social media platforms like Facebook, Twitter, Google+, YouTube, and blogs to address contentious issues head-on. For example, President Paul LeBlanc of Southern New Hampshire University uses his blog to address certain controversial issues because there are no limits on what or how much content he shares there, and people recognize its authority since it is housed on his institution's website. In some cases, college or university presidents will use social media to share their institution's perspective on a particular issue or to invite those stakeholders who have a problem to meet in person to discuss matters further. Whichever approach a higher ed leader takes in terms of whether to acknowledge contentious issues on social media, it cannot be disputed that it is a decision only the president in question can make.

SHARING PERSONAL INFORMATION

The question of how much personal information to reveal on social media was another matter on which presidents held diverging views. The decision to share information about your family, personal life, vacations, or other personal matters on your social media account is up to you. Some of the presidents I interviewed felt sharing elements of their personal lives helped to humanize them as leaders, while others shared no personal information out of a desire to protect their privacy and that of their families. Regardless of whether they share such elements of their personal lives, most college or university leaders' social media content is primarily tied to their roles and their institutions and not their lives outside of those two worlds. As an example, one president cited a proportion of about 80 percent professional and 20 percent personal content.

TAKING A PUBLIC STAND

Some presidents I spoke to believed that the culture and style of their institution and its senior leadership should determine whether they would be more apt to take a public stand on an issue they believed in. Others said they felt that using social media to express strong opinions is a presidential prerogative. Within an institutional culture where the president is expected to be outspoken and a strong advocate for the institution, the president's social media presence ought to reflect that. Alternatively, in an institutional culture where the president's role is one that is perceived as more con-servative, the social media account might reflect that persona. More than half of all the presidents I spoke to believed that presidential social media accounts could become platforms through which to take strong positions on behalf of institutional interests, even in the face of opposition from other social media voices. Before taking a strong stand on a particular issue, a higher ed leader should consider the repercussions of doing so and assess whether the benefits outweigh the costs. The decision of whether to take a public stand is yet another personal choice that every higher ed leader on social media must make at some point or another.

STAYING POSITIVE

Some higher ed leaders choose to use social media to focus on the positive stories about their campuses and their work. They will celebrate institution-al achievements and engage with students about how great their institution is, but they will not touch controversial subjects with a 10-foot pole. Once again, this falls under a president's prerogative. Maintaining a positive and

lighthearted tone in terms of your social media engagement can help ensure followers and stakeholders recognize how passionate and excited you
are about your position. At the same time, conveniently avoiding hot-button
issues relating to your institution might decrease your perceived credibility,
transparency, and trust. Avoiding the tough issues could also lead to the ap-
pearance of a leadership void and lack of accountability at the top of your
institution.

SOCIALIZING WITH STUDENTS

As mentioned, some higher ed leaders are careful about their engagement
on social media, with students in particular, to avoid any compromising situations or accusations of impropriety. The ground rules for some presidents
are steadfast: No direct messaging or following of students. Others take a
more casual approach, regularly communicating, both publicly and privately,
with student stakeholders across social media. While this decision is, as
always, a personal one for a higher ed leader, it may also be influenced by
specific policies or regulations at the institution when it comes to appropriate or inappropriate conduct with respect to communicating with students.
A college or university president must also be careful not to appear to demonstrate nepotism, favoritism, or bias in whom they choose or don't choose
to engage with on social media.

STAYING AWAY FROM INSTITUTIONAL POLITICS

When it comes to what they share on social media about the internal politics and machinations of their institutions, some higher ed leaders abide by
the old adage: Don't air dirty laundry in public. A number of the presidents
I spoke to believed that social media is not the venue for discussing the
institution's internal operations and decision-making unless there is a clear
public need to address the matter. From labor issues and collective bargain-
ing to personnel matters and project delays, a president must decide which
issues to discuss publicly on social media and which matters to keep internal. The key aspect of assessing whether a particular internal matter should
be addressed publicly involves evaluating how it can potentially affect your
key stakeholders. If the issue could attract negative public or media attention to the institution, it may be best to proactively and preemptively address the matter through social and non-social media channels. If the issue
affects few if any stakeholders outside the college or university, it might be
appropriate to keep the matter internal. Often, these situations need to be
evaluated on a case-by-case basis.

#YOUROWNCHOICE

Once you have identified your social media rules of engagement, document the results and keep them handy (e.g., in the notes on your smartphone or posted next to your desktop monitor). Revisiting your personal rules will help keep you on track when you are engaging on social media and help to ensure you're discussing the issues you intended to. Your rules of engagement may change over time, but recognize that this is all part of the process of you becoming a social-media-active higher ed leader.

STRATEGIC ADVISER'S SHARE

• Work with your president to identify what his rules of engagement might be. What issues would he be comfortable discussing on social media, and which does he wish to stay away from?

• What are the perceived ground rules of her social media role models? Can any of these be applied to your president?

• A president's rules of engagement are his prerogative, so be supportive of whatever decisions he makes here.

• Document your president's social media rules of engagement for future reference and to help keep her on track when she goes live on her social network of choice.

PRESIDENT'S POST

• Work with your strategic advisers to develop your social media rules of engagement. What are the topics you wish to discuss and avoid through your social media profile? What subjects do your social media role models discuss or avoid?

• Take note that your social media rules of engagement may evolve over time as you have successes and failures discussing issues with stakeholders across social media.

• Keep your social media rules of engagement handy to ensure you don't lose focus of the issues you wish to bring front and center on social media as well as the topics you wish to stay away from.

Chapter 8

—

#MovingTheNeedle

What are you looking to achieve out of your social media engagement? Some higher ed leaders make the mistake of joining a social network without asking that critical question and are often disappointed by their lackluster results. Establishing your presence on social media because your counterparts are there is all well and good, but when you don't ask yourself what you're looking to get out of it, you risk getting nothing out of it.

Before venturing into social media, college and university presidents need to identify exactly what personal, professional, and institutional interests and priorities they hope to advance through their engagement. Then, by identifying key objectives and metrics, you can ensure that your communications and interactions through social media are serving those larger purposes. You can later use these guiding objectives as a way to measure your social media effectiveness by evaluating whether your engagement has helped to advance these initiatives in any particular way.

One common mistake higher ed leaders make on social media is measuring their effectiveness solely against metrics such as Facebook "likes" and Twitter followers. But are those true measures of social media success and effectiveness? While they may be indicators of how stakeholders are responding to your engagement efforts, those metrics don't measure the impact your social media activity might be having on your institutional priorities. Alternatively, it is advisable to design a success matrix, specific to your own goals, based on metrics that both you and your strategic adviser agree represent value to your college or university. These metrics might include the number of new strategic relationships formed through social media or the number of student questions or comments responded to. These metrics ought to be tied to the institutional priorities and interests that presidential social media engagement is responsible for advancing. All higher ed leaders on social media are looking to move the needle for their institution in one manner or another. So, what needles are you looking to move?

Another common mistake made by higher ed leaders is failing to set a timeline for achieving the social media goals they have in mind. Setting a target date by which a goal ought to be achieved will enable you to have a clearer picture in your mind of what you're working toward. Having a target completion date will also enable you to work with your strategic advisers to check your progress at an agreed-upon midway point and make course corrections as needed. Setting a timeline along with specific and measurable objectives—for example, to engage with 10 current and prospective students per month in order to support your institutional mandate of improved customer service—will set you up to easily evaluate whether you've achieved your social media goals.

In this chapter, we'll identify some potential ways to measure your success on social media while aligning those measures with institutional priorities.

SUPPORTING STRATEGIC PRIORITIES

Whatever your institutional priorities may be, your social media activities can support and align with them. Your institution may be looking to launch a new capital campaign, develop new and relevant programs, or launch a college-wide employee engagement program; whatever the case, your social media engagement can help to advance those plans. The key to successfully aligning activities and priorities is to ask yourself, how are these social media activities helping me to further our institutional goals? If you cannot link your social media engagement to your strategic goals, then it likely will be unable to help you make a measurable impact.

Examples

- Promote our new capital campaign twice a week for six months, and engage with potential donors at least once a day.

- Twice a year, host a virtual town hall on employee engagement through Google+.

- Once a month for three months, showcase a new institutional program offering to industry associations on Twitter.

ENHANCING STAKEHOLDER RELATIONSHIPS

You can evaluate how social media engagement with key stakeholders—including students (both prospective and current), staff, faculty, alumni, media, government officials, donors, and partners—has affected those relationships. Have the relationships been strengthened or enhanced in any way by your interactions on social media? Have your interactions with those stakeholder groups increased as a result of your presence on social media? Has the number of stakeholders you engage with increased? How have those relationships helped you in your role as a college or university president to advance strategic or institutional priorities? Perhaps your social media interactions have led to in-person or telephone meetings with key stakeholders, or maybe helped pave the way for new partnership opportunities, initiatives, or media coverage. If your social media engagement has had no measurable impact on any stakeholder relationship or related institutional outcomes, you are advised to reevaluate your approach. As a reminder, the social media objectives you set should align with strategic priorities and should have target completion dates or timelines attached to them.

Examples

- Interact with local media 10 times over a period of three months to generate greater exposure for the institution.

- Interact with five current students each week to support our strategic customer service initiative.

- Engage with five new potential corporate partners over a six-month period about applied research collaborations linked to our strategic priority of increasing institutional-industry partnerships.

- Liaise with 15 faculty members over a three-month span to improve relations between administration and faculty.

ALTERING INSTITUTIONAL PERCEPTIONS

Your social media goals might also be tied to improving or ameliorating reputational perceptions of your institution. Perhaps you are looking to increase media coverage or rankings in higher ed publications, or maybe your institution has set an internal target of increasing key performance indicators tied to student or employer satisfaction. Setting specific social media objectives tied to these goals will enable you to assess whether you are helping or hindering these causes through your activities online.

Examples

- Pitch five institutional success stories to media over a three-month period to improve our institutional reputation.

- Promote three innovative faculty research projects across social media per month as part of our plan to increase research funding and support.

- Engage with five high-achieving alumni across social media over a three-month period to highlight the institution's recent track record of student success.

INCREASING INSTITUTIONAL MORALE

You or your institution may be looking to increase institutional morale or school spirit, and your social media engagement can help to support that priority too. Higher ed leaders like Santa Ono, Paul LeBlanc, and Elizabeth Stroble do a great job of celebrating what makes their institutions special by celebrating achievements and sharing those stories with their social media followers. Earlier in the book, I told you about Ono's #HottestCollegeInAmerica campaign, but other presidents find individual ways to showcase why theirs is a great institution. Here's a tweet from LeBlanc about an employee morale-boosting activity his team had planned:

@snhuprez: SNHU has reserved a theater for employees to bring their families for premier of last Harry Potter movie.

Whatever you choose to celebrate about the institution, it is clear that sharing these stories on social media can help you galvanize your community and boost perceptions of your institution.

Examples

- Share "five great things" about the university every week for a month.

- Post photos on Instagram highlighting the beauty of the campus twice monthly.

- Profile a new member of the campus community weekly to demonstrate the great and unique students and faculty who are part of the institution.

ADVANCING PROFESSIONAL POSITIONING

The goals you set for your social media engagement may also reflect your own career ambitions or goals. Perhaps you are looking to write and share thought leadership content with your followers, or you wish to highlight the great work you're doing at your institution to set the foundation for a move to another organization. Your social media profile can help you to achieve those goals by providing you with a platform through which to showcase what makes your leadership different and effective. In some cases, you can do so indirectly by sharing words of encouragement that your students and other stakeholders offer to you.

Examples

- Highlight an institutional achievement that has taken place under my leadership tenure once every six months.

- Retweet words of encouragement and congratulations from institutional stakeholders on an ad hoc basis.

- Write and share one blog post monthly on a different thought leadership topic.

- Work with strategic advisers and communications staff to produce an annual "state of the college " YouTube video highlighting organizational successes I have led.

#YOUROWNCHOICE

Not all social media engagement has to be measured against strategic or personal goals. The nature of social media calls for organic and authentic conversations that are sometimes just simply about having fun, sharing unique content, and connecting socially with friends and colleagues. However, higher ed leaders looking to use social media engagement to move the needle on their own and their institution's biggest priorities must find a way to blend their organic conversations with strategically driven content. By aligning your goals and your engagement, you can ensure your social media activities help you in your capacity as a college or university president and help you to move the needle for your institution.

STRATEGIC ADVISER'S SHARE

- Work with your president to identify what her social media objectives are. How do these objectives align with organizational goals and priorities? What is your president hoping to achieve for herself through her social media engagement?

- Collaborate with your president to develop social media engagement activities that could support your goals.

PRESIDENT'S POST

- Honestly ask yourself what you're looking to achieve from your social media engagement. How can your social media activities help to support or advance institutional interests? How can those activities help you to advance your career prospects and professional reputation?

- Work with a strategic adviser or communications staff to develop a list of your social media goals and objectives.

- Ensure that your objectives and tactics are specific and have a set completion date. How many new strategic relationships are you looking to form, and by what date? How many alumni stories are you looking to share, and by what date? Setting specific objectives and timelines will help to keep you on track with respect to actually achieving them.

SOCIAL PROFILE: @WEBSTERPRES

Dr. Elizabeth Stroble, President, Webster University

BIO IN BRIEF

- Named president of Webster University in St. Louis, Mo., in 2009

- Earned a bachelor's degree in history and English from Augustana College; two master's degrees, one in history and one in American and English literature, both from Southern Illinois University–Edwardsville; and a doctorate in curriculum studies from the University of Virginia

- An early adopter of new technology, has been recognized nationally for the leadership role she takes in using social media

- Led Webster in completing the largest comprehensive capital campaign in its history, more than doubling its endowment, and significantly increasing scholarship support for students

- Currently active on Twitter, Facebook, LinkedIn

Source: Webster University website (http://www.webster.edu/president/university-leadership/past-presidents.html)

SOCIAL QUOTES

On accessing a wide range of perspectives: "[Social media] suits my style of communication and community building quite well … I pick pieces and parts of stories about our people, our places, and I spread them out for other members of our community to know. And then my other major communication role that I have taken on as president is translating our stories out to a larger world, whether it be alums or leaders in the communities, or possible donors, or thought leaders, so I'm getting our story out in ways that make it easier to reach those people. And then I'm scanning that external environment and learning more about public policy issues, leadership opportunities, ways that our internal community needs to not only respond but lead in partnership. Social media makes that very immediate and spontaneous and gives access to a wide range of perspectives, opinions, sources—and you can do it quickly without tremendous effort. For me, it's pure fun."

On the question of necessity: "For me, it's a personal and professional necessity. Is it part of what we could ultimately see as a measure of effectiveness of leadership? I think it will ultimately get there. Right now, it's probably a differentiator."

GREATEST SOCIAL TRAITS

Community leadership. Part of what makes Stroble's social media engagement strategy so effective is that she celebrates her role as a community leader in the St. Louis region. Stroble shares photos from the events she attends at her institution but also looks beyond her campus borders to engage in conversations related to the causes she supports in her community. Her personal social media accounts also complement content coming out of Webster's institutional accounts, either through retweets or endorsements of information emanating from those accounts. Stroble's commitment to community causes demonstrates to her followers that she is not solely committed to all things Webster, but that her interests and passions are diverse, and that indirectly her institution is also committed to supporting community interests. Her social media presence can serve as a role model to other presidential accounts in that she often takes the initiative to promote causes of importance to her community, in some cases scooping other local sources.

Personal sharing. Along with content related to her institution and community-based causes, Stroble also mixes in personal content to the stories she shares via social media. Her accounts are not littered with vacation photos or images of what she had for lunch, but she often shares highlights from her personal or social life, such as articles about her favorite TV shows or sporting events she is following. These glimpses of her personal interests serve to humanize her as a president and community leader, and make following her updates something that might appeal to those looking for more than just thought leadership content and institutional news. Stroble's unique mix of content offerings make hers a compelling social media presence and give us an authentic window into her personality.

Engaging with diverse accounts. Whether they are community leaders, reporters, students, faculty, or members of another stakeholder group, Stroble makes an effort to engage with a wide range of people through her social media accounts. What makes her approach unusual is that she engages with individuals with no direct ties or clear vested interest in Webster University. Her social media persona is not solely one of an institutional promoter, but rather a community aggregator, sharing content about and conversing on a variety of issues and groups relevant to her local and national followers. Some presidents on social media only engage with stakeholders close to home—people based within their institutions or whom they know personally or professionally. Stroble engages with most followers regardless of their relationship to her or her institution, and it serves her well with respect to her reputation on and outside of social media.

Chapter 9

—

#DevelopYourStrategy

The best laid plans ... can sometimes get you exactly where you need to be.

That much is true for higher ed leaders on social media, at least. Without a plan for your social media engagement, you're lost, a rudderless boat in a sea of directionless social media accounts. But with a plan, you know exactly where you're going, how long it will take, and how you're going to get there. So, what's in your social media game plan? What is your social media strategy?

College or university presidents are advised to work with strategic advisers or communications staff to develop a personal social media strategy that will guide the types of engagement that take place through their presidential accounts. These strategies are often very specific to particular presidents and their institutions. For some, their strategic social media plans may involve reaching out and strengthening key internal and external stakeholder relationships; for others, their strategy might be tied to promoting student and faculty achievements and successes. While many of the higher ed leaders I interviewed had not developed personal social media strategies, they expressed an interest in doing so, believing such a document could help them come closer to achieving their engagement objectives. Developing a social media strategy is a personal choice for a president, as some may consider such an approach too scripted and inauthentic for the social media channel they wish to embrace, but for most presidents it can serve as a valuable tool to guide their social media engagement.

This document, in which you and your team identify social media priorities, objectives, tactics, supporting resources, measurement tools, crisis readiness plans, and content and event schedules, can provide direction to your social media activities and ensure they align with institutional goals. Each social media strategy document can serve as an outlook on a president's year in social media, but if planning a whole year's worth of social media activity seems overtly ambitious, feel free to develop a quarterly or semiannual plan.

This chapter breaks down the key actions and elements required to develop an effective personal social media strategy document.

SET KEY PRIORITIES

Your social media strategy should begin with the priorities you wish to advance, support, or achieve through social media. Your personal social media priorities don't have to be vague, broad, or high-minded; they just need to reflect the thinking behind the actions you will be taking. Your priorities will guide your objectives, but should not themselves be tangible, tactical actions that you're thinking of employing.

Examples

- Increase reputational perceptions of our institution among social media stakeholders.

- Strengthen strategic relationships with government officials.

- Broaden awareness of our campus's applied research projects.

OUTLINE OBJECTIVES AND TACTICS

As discussed in Chapter 8, your social media strategy should contain a complete list of the objectives you intend to accomplish. This is the place to describe the tangible steps you intend to take to achieve your more general social media priorities. Whatever your objectives, they should contain specific tactics, targets, and completion dates to ensure accountability: What specific activities will you engage in on social media? What specific actions will you take?

Examples

- Support improved student satisfaction efforts by responding to three student queries on Twitter daily for three months.

- Enhance alumni relationships by reaching out to one high-profile graduate on Facebook once a month for six months.

- Support our employee engagement campaign by highlighting the institution's efforts, with images and videos shared on Instagram, once a week for six months.

PREPARE A SUCCESS MATRIX

Create a table within which your social media priorities, objectives, tactics, targets, and completion dates are all easily accessible and on display. This can be a portion of your strategy that you revisit regularly to ensure your activities are squarely in line with your goals. Your social media success matrix by no means has to look exactly like the one displayed below, but it should be an accurate reflection of what you're looking to accomplish on social media and how you're going to get there.

Sample Social Media Success Matrix

PRIORITIES	Enhance alumni relationships	Boost school spirit	Support employee engagement	Improve customer service satisfaction
OBJECTIVES	Strengthen ties with high-profile alumni on social media	Celebrate institutional success stories	Identify new opportunities to engage with employees	Set institutional tone for renewed commitment to serving our students
TACTICS	Engage and reach out to high-profile alumni	Share latest news and achievements from our institution	Discuss ways to involve employees in organizational decision-making	Respond to student queries through my personal account
TARGETS	Complete three alumni engagement activities on social media every month	Share one institutional achievement daily on social media for three months	Reach out to three employees every week and discuss employee engagement issues for six months	Respond to five student queries daily and delegate to appropriate departments as needed for one year
COMPLETION DATE	February 2016	Revisit in January 2016	March 2016	April 2017
PLATFORMS	Facebook	LinkedIn	Google+	Twitter

IDENTIFY SUPPORTING RESOURCES

Which members of your staff will assist you with your social media engagement? Develop a list of your social media support team. Are these people based solely in the Office of the President, or are they members of your communications staff as well? Find individuals who are well connected across your institution, people who are familiar with social media, who can serve as strategic advisers and keep you abreast of issues and events happening across your campus community. Having the list of social media support staff readily available will make responding to pressing issues easier, more effective, and more efficient. Be sure to give each member of your support team a specific role. Some individuals might be dedicated to actively monitoring issues and keywords, while others might be your go-to sources for information about institutional events or specific stakeholder groups.

Examples

• Director of Communications: Shares college events and happenings on a weekly basis.

- Executive Director, Office of the President: Actively monitors relevant issues being discussed on social media and provides a report every two weeks.

- Director of Alumni Relations: Actively seeks out social-media-active alumni and provides a monthly summary.

- Digital/Social Media Manager: Measures social media outcomes and provides support and information on emerging social media platforms, trends, conventions, and movements on an ad hoc basis.

SELECT MEASUREMENT TOOLS AND METRICS

Depending on what your social media objectives are, you and your strategic advisers may wish to use some measurement tools to track who is following your account and with whom you are engaging. While Facebook has a built-in "insights" tool that enables you to view who your followers are and where they are located, you may wish to use paid monitoring and measurement services like Sprout Social, Salesforce's Radian6, and Sysomos' Heartbeat to keep track of your social media engagement metrics. These tools are often best managed by your institution's web or communications staff, specifically, your digital or social media manager, who should then report results regularly to the president. Delegation of these measurement responsibilities is particularly important, since as a higher ed leader, you are likely already struggling to find time to engage on social media in the first place. If you are measuring your social media success based on less tangible metrics, you or an adviser may be forced to track your progress manually. Less tangible metrics tied to your personal social media strategy might include the number of new stakeholder relationships formed; the number of employee engagement interactions; or the number of new applied research partnerships originating from social media. Below are some more examples of measurable metrics that higher ed leaders on social media might keep track of.

Examples

- Number of in-person meetings with government officials resulting from social media engagement.

- Percentage increase in employee engagement ratings resulting from social media activities.

- Number of local media stories stemming from social media engagement.

DEVELOP CRISIS READINESS AND RISK MANAGEMENT PLANS

One of the most crucial elements of your social media strategy is your crisis communications and risk management documentation. The more proactive you are in preparing for potential issues that you or your institution may face on social media, the more effective you will be in leading your institution past those issues. The crisis readiness plan will contain key messaging and content to share with followers through your social media account in the event of an emergency. Meanwhile, the risk management plan will address common or recurring issues specific to your social media engagement and offer messaging to address those scenarios. These plans will prepare you for a variety of situations relating to your personal social media presence, including having your account hacked, being impersonated on social media, an emergency situation on campus, or a recurring issue specific to you or your campus that has previously reared its head on social media. In the tables below, you will find examples of how you might structure such plans.

Sample Crisis Readiness Plan

CRISIS SCENARIO	KEY MESSAGES	FREQUENTLY ASKED QUESTIONS	SOCIAL MEDIA–SPECIFIC MESSAGING
Lockdown on campus	Please remain where you are until local authorities and campus security have declared an all-clear.	President Zaiontz, where should I go on campus in the event of an emergency?	The school is in lockdown. Remain calm and stay where you are until you get an all-clear from campus security or police. #Emergency [Twitter]
Blackout on campus	Our facilities team is currently working with local power authorities to restore service to the campus.	President Zaiontz, the power is out across the college. What is being done about this?	We are aware of the power disruption on campus. We are working w/ local power authorities to resolve the issue. Stay tuned for updates. [Twitter]

Sample Risk Management Plan

ISSUE	KEY MESSAGES	FREQUENTLY ASKED QUESTIONS	SOCIAL MEDIA–SPECIFIC MESSAGING
President's account is being impersonated	Please ignore all content coming from @PrezZaiontz. This is an imposter account.	@PresZaiontz, why are you saying all these inappropriate things on social media?	Please ignore @ PrezZaiontz. It's an imposter account. You can continue to follow the real me @PresZaiontz. I've informed Twitter about this. [Twitter]
College employees publicly share frustrations over fiscal austerity measures	Due to a challenging economic climate, the college has had to make some difficult decisions about its expenditures and find reasonable fiscal efficiencies where possible.	How does college leadership account for the hiring of mostly contract faculty and the cutting of humanities course offerings this term?	I invite any college employee with questions about our budgeting decisions to meet with me in person in the coming days. Email me directly and we'll make arrangements to chat. Furthermore, we will be hosting a virtual town hall on the subject of "College Budgeting in a Challenging Fiscal Climate" next week, to which all staff and students are invited. Click on the link below to register: https://plus.google. com/+ZaiontzCollege [Google+]

CREATE A CONTENT CALENDAR

Your social media game plan should also contain a content calendar through which you can keep track of events and happenings on campus and identify points in time when you wish to share content on social media. This calendar can be a collaborative effort between you and your strategic advisers as well as your communications staff. The content calendar should not serve as a script for social media content, but rather should work like a gentle reminder of the different content you might wish to discuss and highlight through your social media profile. In the calendar below, you will see examples of items that you might wish to highlight in a content calendar and share on social media.

Sample Content Calendar

— September 2016 —

SUN	MON	TUE	WED	THU	FRI	SAT
				1 Staff town hall event	2 Interview with *U.S. News & World Report* school rankings reporter	3
4	5 Labor Day	6 First day of fall classes	7 Fall Orientation / Freshman Welcome	8 Fall Orientation / Freshman Welcome	9 President's Welcome Ceremony	10
11 Faculty Welcome Back BBQ	12 Applied Research Day	13 Career Fair	14 Social Media Conference on campus	15 New program launch event	16 Varsity women's soccer home opener	17 College golf tournament
18	19 Welcome speech to Student Union	20 Board of Governors meeting	21 Student Animation Film Festival on campus	22 Local Business Forum on campus	23 Varsity men's basketball home opener	24 Cancer Research Walk on campus
25	26 Mayor's visit	27 Fall Harvest Festival on campus	28 Official opening of new Image Arts Building	29 Canadian dignitaries on campus	30 Alumni speaker series	

REVISIT THE GAME PLAN

Work with a strategic adviser to set regular intervals in which you will revisit your social media strategic plan to check on your progress and reevaluate objectives, social media channels, tactics, targets, and timelines. You and their teams can also use these sessions to correct course as needed, as well as to check in on progress (or lack thereof) toward reaching targeted and measurable metrics identified within the plan. The following proposed check-in schedule could support a president whose team has developed a yearlong social media strategy. This schedule does not include the regular day-to-day support that a president may have requested with respect to receiving institutional news and event updates or social media monitoring reports. (For more on these meetings, see Chapter 12.)

Proposed check-in timeline

- September 2016: President's social media plan is established.
- October 2016: Check-in meeting #1.
- December 2016: Check-in meeting #2.
- March 2017: Check-in meeting #3.
- June 2017: Check-in meeting #4.
- September 2017: Reevaluate and update social media plan.

#YOUROWNCHOICE

Once again, developing a personal social media strategy is not a requirement for achieving success or advancing institutional interests, but it can help to keep you focused on the objectives that are most important to you. These documents can be as specific or general as you or your strategic adviser sees fit; the most important factor is that as the president whose social media account is being strategized, you are comfortable with the game plan being put in place.

STRATEGIC ADVISER'S SHARE

- If your president is interested in developing a personal social media strategy, work with him to create and develop the document. Talk with your president about his social media priorities and objectives and how they might align with your institution's strategic goals.

- Make the necessary preparations to ensure you and your president have the resources readily available to collaboratively develop her social media strategy. This might include a college events calendar, your institution's strategic plan document, your crisis communications plan, and any other documents you think might be helpful for the planning process.

PRESIDENT'S POST

- Assess whether you think a personal social media strategy could be something that might help you to achieve your objectives as well as advance your institutional interests.

- Work collaboratively with your strategic advisers to develop a social media plan that aligns with your schedule, communications style, and personality. Don't commit to any activities that you feel uncomfortable with or do not fully understand; this is, after all, your social media profile we're talking about.

- Recognize that this document will evolve over time. Some of the activities in this document will succeed while others will not, but you and your advisers need to accept this as part of the process of refining your social media approach.

- Whether yours is a quarterly or annual plan, ensure you are regularly self-assessing, checking in, and correcting course as you see fit.

Next Steps

Chapter 10

—

#PutARingOnIt

In this book, I've compared social media to a lot of things: buying a car, navigating a boat, and now, working out at the gym. Social media is a lot like working out. If you don't commit to it, you won't see results. This concept also makes me think of Beyoncé's lyric: "If you liked it, then you should've put a ring on it." Pretty spot on with respect to social media, too. Thus this chapter's title.

The importance, for a higher ed leader, of committing to keeping a social media account active is an undeniable best practice and a recommendation emerging from my research. Social networks are littered with abandoned social media accounts of college or university presidents who were inattentive to their online constituents and whose ventures onto those networks were particularly ineffective.

If you find you are no longer interested in engaging on a particular social network, I would advise you to delete your account rather than abandon it. By contrast, if you wish to effectively and strategically communicate with key stakeholders and advance institutional interests, I'd advise you to actively populate your account with content and engage with constituents, stakeholders, and followers consistently.

Research suggests that organizational leaders do not necessarily recognize the importance of making a commitment to social media or see social media engagement as an opportunity to become a more involved and informed leader. An April 2012 Wall Street Journal article by Alexandra Samuel explained the problem with the way many organizational leaders perceive social media and the kind of paradigm shift that might be required in their thinking: "The solution is to stop looking at social media as another platform you have to learn—yet another responsibility—and start seeing it for what it can be instead: a personal toolbox for improving your practice of leadership." Senior leaders who have achieved success using social media are often individuals who have genuinely embraced the tools and have a sincere desire to use stakeholder feedback to inform their organizational decision-making. Effective social media engagement is often difficult to achieve when a leader considers such engagement an arduous activity rather than evaluating the potential opportunities that activity could generate.

This chapter will offer you some tips on staying committed to your social media engagement while also allowing you the opportunity to give it the boot if it no longer fits into your life.

CHECKING IN WITH STRATEGIC ADVISERS

The importance of checking in with strategic advisers and communications staff to evaluate and assess your social media efforts cannot be underscored enough. These meetings could also help to keep you committed to social media efforts. Perhaps, in the early going, your follower numbers are low or your engagement with internal stakeholders is more negative than positive. These check-in meetings can help you talk through the issues you are experiencing on social media and allow the team to troubleshoot potential solutions. Many of the presidents I spoke with talked about initially thinking they might quit social media altogether because theirs was an isolated experience with little support offered (or sought) from their institutional staff. (For more on these meetings, see Chapter 12.)

ESTABLISHING GOALPOSTS

In Chapter 9 and above, I advised higher ed leaders to work with their strategic advisers to schedule meetings at which the social media advisory team could huddle together, assess the progress made to date, and evaluate whether they need to make any changes to their social media strategy. In addition to those meetings, I would advise setting goalposts for your social media engagement. These are different from the objectives or goals you identify in your social media plan. Instead, a goalpost reflects progress you've made toward a particular objective before you reach the targeted completion date. These goalposts can align with your check-in meetings, or they can operate on a separate timeline tied specifically to the objective they are supporting. For instance, if you have set the objective of increasing alumni engagement and you intend to develop 20 new alumni relationships via social media by September 2016, your goalposts could be spread across the time between the present and your target completion date, enabling you to track your progress and reevaluate your approach. Monitoring your progress through goalposts can help to keep you motivated (also kind of like working out!) to continue engaging on social media, as you are able to view the progress you're making on your way to the goal you've set. See another example of goalposts being employed and documented on the following page.

Sample Goalposts

Objective: Enhance employee engagement
Strategy: Engage with employees via social media
Tactics: Tweet with employees daily
Target: Engage on social media with 300 employees by September 2016
Project start date: January 2016

DATE	GOALPOST	# OF ACTUAL EMPLOYEE INTERACTIONS	COURSE CORRECTION
March 2016	50	45	President began engaging employees on Facebook and Twitter
June 2016	100	150	
August 2016	200	300	
September 2016	300	350	

TIME COMMITMENT

Ask yourself: Have you made the time to fit social media into your life?

Some of the social-media-active presidents I spoke to carved out a social media zone in their daily agendas, which they devoted solely to responding to inquiries and sharing content on their social media accounts. Whether you are carving out time in the morning or checking in on social media throughout the day, it is important to assess whether you've made the tangible time commitment to support your social media activities. If you are struggling to do that, the next tip might help.

SCHEDULING CONTENT

Some higher ed leaders have embraced content scheduling tools to feed updates to their social media accounts even when they are away from their mobile devices or computers. Content scheduling/management tools like Hootsuite and Tweetdeck enable you to connect multiple social media profiles to one web-based interface and schedule tweets, Facebook statuses, Google+ posts, and LinkedIn updates to go out on specific dates at specific times in the future. While these scheduled posts cannot replace real-time engagement on social media, they can help to keep your account active and populated when your schedule gets busy. A few words of warning about relying too heavily on scheduled posts through these tools: First and foremost, social media effectiveness relies on two-way engagement, and that cannot happen if you are not engaging with stakeholders and are merely relying on scheduled content to be published on your behalf. Secondly, if you are promoting time-sensitive activities or events through social media and there is a change in venue or time information at the last minute, a scheduled post with outdated information can hurt your social media reputation. The lesson? Ensure all scheduled content is both up-to-date and accurate.

#YOUROWNCHOICE

Honestly assess whether social media is really something you're ready to commit to at this point. If you feel the potential opportunities are worth the investment of time required, then make the decision that you will actively devote time to engaging with your social media stakeholders. If, however, you have reevaluated your schedule, responsibilities, and level of interest in social media, own that, and delete your social media profile.

STRATEGIC ADVISER'S SHARE

- Discuss how you can better support your president's social media engagement efforts, and help her commit to the account she has launched.

- Schedule and arrange check-in meetings with your president to evaluate the social media strategy you've collaboratively developed, assess progress to date, and make any changes you both deem appropriate.

- Work with your president to identify goalposts tied to the objectives he has set. How is he currently tracking his progress?

- Share information about content scheduling/management tools like Hootsuite and Tweetdeck and see if that might help her to keep her accounts active and populated with content.

PRESIDENT'S POST

- Ask yourself if you are dedicating a sufficient amount of time to support your social media activities through the course of your day. Do you have time blocked out each day to engage on social media?

- Are you regularly checking in with your strategic advisers and support staff to assess whether your personal social media strategy is working in the way you envisioned?

- Make the decision to either continue engaging on social media or quit altogether. Do not waver here. A president with an inactive social media account can harm professional and institutional reputations more than a president with no social media profile at all.

Chapter 11

—

#HelpWanted

Up to this point, we have made a big assumption. And you know what happens when one assumes.

I've assumed that the higher ed leaders reading this book have some help in terms of supporting their social media engagement efforts. But that may not be the case for some of you.

I assure you, it wasn't my intention to make an ass out of you or me. But the reason that strategic advisers are featured so prominently in this book is that higher ed leaders on social media need all the help they can get in order to be effective. Which leads me to this chapter's recommendation: Get some help!

It was one of the best practices that emanated from my research. Higher ed leaders on social media benefited immensely when their activities were supported by advisers, whether from the institution's own Office of the President, communications staff, or digital teams, or from external agencies. We've talked a lot in this book about what some of that support might look like. Perhaps it involves providing the president with a steady stream of potential stories to share through his social media channels, or giving her honest and critical feedback about ways she can enhance her social media engagement, or being the second set of eyes monitoring his personal social media accounts. Social media advisers, referred to throughout this book as strategic advisers, can warn presidents about potential issues, controversies, or questions needing or waiting to be addressed by key constituents. The latter support is particularly valuable to presidents concerned that their busy schedules will not allow them to effectively monitor social media for potential risks and opportunities.

Strategic advisers can be invaluable in supporting college or university presidents in their social media forays and engagement. A strategic adviser can be any professional with an understanding of communications and social media best practices, social media channels, and institutional strategic objectives. More than anything else, a strategic adviser must also be a trusted adviser to a higher ed leader, on whom who the president can rely for honesty, candor, and practical advice.

Many of the presidents I spoke to were looking for strategic support from their communications teams, and they often reported that few individuals were stepping up to help them in their engagement activities. Was it a fear of offending a senior leader? A lack of social media expertise within the Office of the President? Whatever the reasons, there are unique opportunities being presented to individuals with social media expertise to collaborate with senior leaders and support their social media efforts.

Another quick takeaway on the issue of supporting higher ed leaders on social media: Most of them drew the line at tactical support. Almost all of the presidents I interviewed wanted to be in control of their social media accounts and looked to advisers to give them honest and tangible guidance that could help them to advance institutional interests. What they were not looking for was someone to write a social media script for them. That is, they wanted advice, not a ghostwriter.

The tips that follow can help you identify strategic advisers and work with them to support your social media engagement efforts.

FIND YOUR STRATEGIC ADVISERS

Whether they reside within the Office of the President, your communications and public relations staff, or your digital team, find the social media experts within your college or university. These may be individuals with active and recognized social media accounts or academics who have researched the subject. Your strategic advisers could also come from outside of your institution. External consultancies, like mStoner Inc., the publisher of this book, can offer social media counsel to higher ed leaders looking for support. Whomever your strategic advisers might be, ensure that they are individuals whom you implicitly trust and who have preferably demonstrated a successful track record of social media expertise, counsel, and support. Some higher ed institutions, including my employer, Seneca College, have launched social media programs, and credentials like that might soon become a requirement for your social media strategic advisers.

CREATE THEIR TO-DO LIST

Once you've determined who your strategic advisers could be, work with them to build a personal social media to-do list. How can these advisers help you in your social media engagement? Here are some examples of things your strategic advisers may be able to do to support you:

• generate a list of social media role models for you to follow

• offer you insights into the conventions, trends, expectations, and common
• practices of various social networks

- collaborate with you to develop your personal social media strategy

- conduct an environmental scan of the issues being discussed on social media that might influence your activities

- offer you content ideas and news or events to share from across your institution

- offer you critical feedback on the strengths and weaknesses of your social media activities

- highlight synergies between your organizational priorities and objectives, your professional goals, and your social media engagement

- counsel you on issues to address or avoid on social media

- serve as a sober second thought on messages or content you wish to share

- support you in your efforts to develop thought leadership content

- identify opportunities to delegate nonessential social media tasks like referring student inquiries to appropriate departments

- monitor your activities and keep you up to date on results you may not be aware of through routine monitoring of institution-related social media activity.

KNOW WHAT THEY KNOW

Work with your strategic advisers to develop knowledge-sharing practices. Identify your areas of weakness and knowledge gaps when it comes to social media, and collaborate to address those areas. Perhaps they are readers of web-based publications like Mashable or Social Media Today, which keep them abreast of the latest social media news, best practices, and platforms. Or maybe they get most of their social media knowledge by observing the social networks themselves. However they may acquire their social media know-how, find ways to absorb as much information from them as possible. It will only improve your own engagement practices and make you more capable of operating independently within the social media environment. There are no stupid questions between you and your strategic advisers. Don't know what a retweet is? Ask your strategic adviser. Can't understand why few people are engaging with you through your account? Ask your strategic adviser. Like anyone embracing a new initiative, responsibility, or process, higher ed leaders need support, and the only way to learn, aside from trial and error, is to look to great teachers.

STRATEGIC ADVISER'S SHARE

- If you think you're a candidate to serve as a strategic adviser to your president, take a chance and reach out to him. Share what makes you a social media expert, describe your social media experiences to date, tell him what you've observed about his social media engagement, and point out opportunities he has yet to capitalize on.

• Presuming she accepts your offer of support, work with your president to identify what you can do to help her. Perhaps she's looking for support in developing content to share through her account, or maybe she's just looking for a second set of eyes to review her social media decision-making. Whatever kind of support she's seeking, find ways to impart your knowledge to her.

PRESIDENT'S POST

• Ask yourself if you think you can benefit from social media support and counsel.

• Explore your internal and external candidates for strategic social media support. Who has the social media expertise, track record, or credentials to work with you? Who within your organization or outside of it do you implicitly trust? Preferably, select strategic advisers who meet both criteria.

• Work with your strategic advisers to develop a game plan for how they might be able to support your social media engagement.

• Learn as much as you can from your strategic advisers. Fill in your social media knowledge gaps, and learn to read what they're reading.

SOCIAL PROFILE: @DOMINIC_GIROUX

Dominic Giroux, President, Laurentian University

BIO IN BRIEF

- Became the tenth president of Laurentian University in Sudbury, Ontario, in April 2009
- Previously served as assistant deputy minister with the Ontario Ministry of Education and the Ministry of Training, Colleges and Universities
- Received one of Canada's "Top 40 Under 40" Awards in 2011 and was named the 2010 Education Personality of the Year by Radio-Canada/Le Droit
- Led Laurentian in achieving record-high enrollment levels while increasing the average entry grade, eliminated a substantial operating deficit, and initiated new capital projects worth more than $140 million (CDN)
- Currently active on Twitter, Facebook, LinkedIn, blog

Source: Laurentian University website (http://laurentian.ca/president-and-vice-chancellor)

SOCIAL QUOTES

On presidents raising important issues: "It has helped put some issues on the radar and get recognition for the university ... It depends on the ethos of each institution, but I think students, faculty, and staff like, every once in a while, when a president says, 'hold on a second here, that's not right.' The community is beginning to expect that from a president … Do it too much, and it doesn't carry as much weight."

On actively listening to your community: "One of the biggest uses of social media is to check … for what people are saying about our institution. I do this at least daily, and I find it just amazing to read about what students are saying positively or negatively about what's going on."

On the relationship between age and a willingness to embrace social media: "I think there may be an age factor here where maybe a president is in his 30s or early 40s, he'll feel more comfortable on social media … Someone who is in their 60s or 70s … may not."

GREATEST SOCIAL TRAITS

The school's storyteller. Much like other presidential accounts, Giroux's social media presence helps to keep his followers abreast of the latest goings-on at Laurentian University, but he also serves as a key resource on the strategic plans and priorities of his institution. Many of the Giroux's updates revolve around the ambitious plans and goals of his institution, from the development of new buildings and partnerships to the achievements of his fellow campus leaders. While Laurentian's institutional account tends to concentrate on internal happenings, events, and initiatives, Giroux's presence on social media takes a higher-level view, with a focus on Laurentian's impact in the context of the local, provincial, and national landscapes. Giroux is a great institutional storyteller, mixing in updates from the day-to-day operations of his institution but also offering a big-picture view to interested parties and stakeholders.

Bilingual communications. Another unusual element of Giroux's social media approach on Twitter and Facebook is his delivery of bilingual content—both English and French—to his followers. Sudbury is a bilingual city in Northern Ontario, so this is an expectation for institutional accounts (Laurentian is a bilingual university), but not necessarily a requirement for Giroux's personal accounts. Giroux, who is fully bilingual himself, not only makes his social media accounts more accessible to followers by offering his content in both English and French, but he also reflects his desire to reach out to a diverse range of stakeholders, regardless of their language, within his community.

Recognizes professional advancement. Giroux has also proven to be consistent in his efforts to recognize the professional success stories of his faculty, staff, and students at Laurentian. Whether acknowledging the achievements of senior leaders across his institution or academic appointments, both internal and external, Giroux uses his social media presence to pat those individuals on the back and ensure they feel recognized by him. Many presidents interviewed as part of my research talked about the value of social media not only to celebrate institutional success stories, but also to recognize specific individuals for a job well done. While this recognition cannot replace an actual pat on the back or in-person acknowledgement, for a president with many pressing time and travel commitments, social media recognition can be a quick, effective, meaningful and public way to boost employee and institutional morale.

SOCIAL PROFILE: @PREZONO

Dr. Santa Ono, President, University of Cincinnati

BIO IN BRIEF

• Has served as president of the University of Cincinnati (UC) in Ohio since August 2012

• Born in Vancouver, earned his Ph.D. at McGill University and his B.A. at the University of Chicago

• A highly accomplished researcher in eye disease and a member of several national and international honor societies

• Has gained a reputation as a chief executive who is accessible and responsive to his university's wide range of stakeholders, including students, faculty, staff, alumni, and parents, as well as business, civic, arts, and government leaders

• Currently active on Twitter, Facebook, Google+, LinkedIn, Instagram

Source: University of Cincinnati website (http://www.uc.edu/president/the-president.html)

SOCIAL QUOTES

On the benefits of social media: "The key benefit to me is that I know more clearly and more quickly what people are thinking, particularly students. UC strives to be student-centered, and this helps me to do that. Students tell me about the great news they've heard, their concerns, issues we need to address. It has also allowed people to get to know me as a person, not just as a president."

On the issue of vulnerability: "The biggest challenge is the vulnerability. Being accessible on social media leaves you open to all comments, both positive and negative. You must be prepared to receive criticism, even from your own kids."

On the content he shares: "I post everything from photos of sunsets to quotes from popular music and news about the latest UC rankings. My social media voice is not much different from my everyday voice in face-to-face conversation, although I guess I don't quote pop music much in person."

Source: Interview with Christopher G. Barrows, Medium.com, March 28, 2014.

GREATEST SOCIAL TRAITS

Institutional champion. Ono is a rock star among higher ed leaders on social media, and part of the reason for this is that he will tell anyone willing to listen about what's happening at the University of Cincinnati. Ono epitomizes an institutional champion: highlighting his university's achievements, both academic and non-academic; interacting with key stakeholders, including students, faculty, staff, alumni, and partners; and also serving as "cheerleader-in-chief" whenever possible. The best example of Ono's efforts to champion his institution were via the #HottestCollegeInAmerica hashtag that he has actively promoted on social media since being appointed in 2012. A true indicator of its effectiveness wasn't Ono consistent use of the hashtag when sharing news about his campus, but rather when his followers began to share it in their updates. Once that happened, current and prospective students as well as stakeholders across his institutional community knew which was the #HottestCollegeInAmerica.

Engages with students. Ono is quite simply one of the best higher ed leaders on social media when it comes to engaging with his students. Whether the conversation is about celebrating an athletic victory or simply encouraging school spirit, Ono has put in a dedicated effort to ensure he not only remains accessible to students but also fosters virtual relationships with them. Ono both responds to student inquiries targeted to him and also enters into conversations with students where he might be able to help or contribute. Shining through even more than his customer service efforts, however, is his sense of humor and genuine enjoyment derived from serving as UC president. By showing his authentic personality through social media, Ono makes it clear that understands that creating a positive student experience is about more than great teaching and learning; it's about building community (something he has often talked about when describing his social media approach).

Community builder. Ono is known for interacting with a broad cross-section of stakeholders through his social media accounts. He is different things to different audiences. To other higher ed leaders, he can be counted on to share his thoughts and positions on policy issues or trends in postsecondary education; to faculty and staff, he celebrates their achievements through recognition and acknowledgement on social media; to students and alumni, he spreads school spirit and addresses their questions and concerns; and through his efforts with these different stakeholder groups, he is able to build stronger linkages and connections that strengthen his own and his institution's reputations and sense of community. Ono has made his social media accounts serve as hubs for the UC community to not only follow his activities and updates but also, through his connections, to learn about and experience all angles of the UC world. He is, in a sense, the tie that binds all those facets together.

Chapter 12

—

#AreWeThereYet

On social media as in life, it's important to stop every once in a while and take stock of what's happened.

As advised in Chapters 9 and 10, it's crucial for higher ed leaders on social media to pause intermittently to evaluate where they are in achieving their goals and assess what's worked and what hasn't. In this chapter, we'll discuss what can be gained by taking a pause and making a course correction.

After a period of time and at regular intervals, higher ed leaders should measure whether they have been able to achieve, in whole or in part, some or all of the objectives they set out to accomplish when they activated their social media account or accounts. The decision to stop and look around might be made based on your personal social media strategy, and be done by yourself or with the help of your strategic advisers.

If little progress has been achieved in advancing social media or institutional goals, evaluate how you might refine your social media activities, approach, and engagement to improve effectiveness and overall results. If objectives appear to be on track or have already been achieved, taking time to check in might enable you and your strategic advisers to identify new opportunities that you could capitalize on with your presidential social media presence.

Below is a proposed agenda for one of these check-in meetings.

WHAT'S THE STATE OF SOCIAL?

The president and strategic advisers will outline how and in what ways they've each contributed to the president's social media engagement efforts to date. Talk about your role and in what capacities you've supported your president.

Discuss where your social media engagement and activities currently stand. What have you been able to accomplish to date? What is your progress on achieving the goals you set out to achieve? What is left to accomplish?

Recap the major engagement activities that have taken place on social media to date through the president's account(s). What response and results did these activities generate?

Identify which priorities and objectives remain relevant to the president and which are of lesser importance. If there are new objectives to bring forward, begin discussing how these priorities can be supported through social media. If there are no changes to a president's social media objectives, then move on.

WHAT WORKED, AND WHAT DIDN'T?

Break down each of your social media strategies and tactics completed to date. Which activities went as expected, and which did not? For the activities that didn't go as expected, what, in your assessment, was its weakness? What might you do differently in the future?

Evaluate which social media engagement practices you intend to carry forward into the future, and which you won't.

Assess which engagement activities can be refined and changed in the future, and which can be abandoned.

Which social media engagement activities can be applied to the new objectives brought forward earlier? How will these activities support the aforementioned objectives and priorities?

Discuss any critical feedback you have to share either about the president's social media engagement practices and habits or the support being provided by the strategic advisers.

WHAT SHOULD WE DO ABOUT IT?

Have the president or the group decide which social media engagement activities will continue as per the personal social media strategy, and which activities will be either added or removed from the plan.

Decide on what other actions to take based on the issues raised thus far. Does the social media strategy need to be revised? Will you experiment with a new social media engagement tactic? Will you stop a particular activity that your plan has called for to date?

Will the president and the group decide to stay the course and make no changes to the personal social media plan?

Discuss any emerging opportunities, issues, social media tools, platforms, trends, and news that could be relevant to the president's engagement efforts. What new activities or social media tools are your higher ed role models embracing? Can these be integrated into your social media strategy? Are there any opportunities to experiment with these new tools or approaches?

NEXT STEPS

Draft a list of post-meeting accountabilities/responsibilities and set target dates for their completion.

Schedule your next check-in meeting as agreed upon by all parties involved.

STRATEGIC ADVISER'S SHARE

• Arrange and schedule regular social media check-in meetings with your president to evaluate the progress of her social media engagement activities.

• What materials, feedback, or information can you bring to these meetings to help make them productive and valuable for your president?

PRESIDENT'S POST

• Identify opportunities to stop and evaluate your social media effectiveness. Ask yourself if you are making progress in achieving the professional or institutional objectives you set out to achieve.

• Work with your strategic adviser to schedule check-in meetings where you analyze all facets of your social media engagement and determine what steps you can take to refine your approach.

SOCIAL PROFILE: @BETHANYCOLLEGE1

Dr. Scott Miller, President, Bethany College

BIO IN BRIEF

• Has served as president of Bethany College in Bethany, W. Va., since 2007

• Has been a college president for almost 25 years, including at Wesley College in Dover, Del., for more than a decade

• Writes regularly for *The Huffington Post*, *College Planning and Management*, *Enrollment Manager*, and *The State Journal*

• Respected as one of the most entrepreneurial higher education executives in America

• Currently active on Twitter, Facebook, LinkedIn, Instagram, Flickr, blog

Source: Bethany College website (http://www.bethanywv.edu/about-bethany/president-and-college-leadership)

SOCIAL QUOTES

On the responsibility of presidents to speak out: "Our college has an experienced president, and people are looking to that experienced president for answers, and so the information that I try to post is what I think an experienced president should do … But I think a lot of presidents fear social media because of the new climate of political correctness … I'm one who believes that college presidents should get up and speak on relevant topics … The great college presidents of our time were known for speaking out on issues, and that's what higher educational leaders should do ... And because of things that have negatively affected leaders, college presidents are shying away from that ... They want scripted responses rather than impromptu discussions."

On the value of social media: "What I've found to be the value in [social media] has been with donors, corporations, and government leaders who follow me, who feel like they have that one-on-one relationship, and as a result, I can cultivate those constituents for a benefit-return for the institution, faster."

On what the future holds: "It is a benefit and it will become a necessity. I'm going to say in five years, you'll see a significant surge in the number of presidents who are engaged on social media."

GREATEST SOCIAL TRAITS

Outspoken style. With a quarter-century of experience as a college president, Miller has the rope and license to share strong opinions on social media without fear of censure—and that he does. Whether his comments focus on budget decisions or trends in higher education, Miller uses his social media presence as a platform through which to express his views, and people listen. He also does an effective job of engaging in thoughtful debate in defense of his positions, never letting the tone of a conversation get too negative, aggressive, or personal. Miller told me that he gives everything he shares on social media a sober second thought to ensure there are limited negative repercussions for him or his institution. At the same time, Miller welcomes opposing viewpoints and responds to those who agree or disagree with him in equal measure. What is refreshing about Miller's social media candor is that few presidents are as open in their positions on contentious issues as he is, particularly in the volatile social media space.

Content aggregator. Miller's social media accounts have become trusted and reliable resources for those of us working in higher education and higher ed leadership. The Bethany College president consistently shares articles, research, and videos (including some content of his own making) pertaining to trending and emerging issues that are relevant to administrators, staff, and faculty working within American academia. Miller's followers have come to recognize and appreciate his knack for finding stories worthy of the attention of higher ed leaders and content relating to best practices. Across different social media platforms, Miller shares diverse content, including infographics and memes on Instagram and article and video links on Twitter. Social media users are drawn to accounts like Miller's because his content is not limited to information about his institution but rather covers a variety of different subject areas.

Targeted engagement. Miller is strategic in his social media engagement and therefore takes a targeted approach in terms of those with whom he engages. With a focus on promoting the brand of his institution, Miller identifies stakeholders whose interests might align with his own (or those of Bethany College), be they potential partners, successful alumni, or prospective students and faculty. While Miller's engagement is not solely limited to these sorts of interactions, he primarily focuses on using his social media accounts to support institutional objectives and priorities. What makes this approach so effective is that success for Miller on social media is not necessarily defined or measured by likes and followers but rather by his ability to advance the goals of his organization through his social media activity. There are certainly higher ed leaders on social media with more followers than Miller, but few who are as influential.

SOCIAL PROFILE: @SNHUPREZ

Dr. Paul LeBlanc, President, Southern New Hampshire University

BIO IN BRIEF

- Became president of Southern New Hampshire University (SNHU) in Manchester, N.H., in 2003

- Served as president of Marlboro College in Marlboro, Vt., from 1996 to 2003

- Won a New England Higher Education Excellence Award in 2012; was listed one of 15 "Classroom Revolutionaries" by *Forbes* and as one of "New Hampshire's Most Influential People" by *New Hampshire Business Review*; and appeared on Bloomberg TV's "Innovators" series

- Led SNHU in becoming the third largest university in the state of New Hampshire and the largest nonprofit provider of online education in the U.S.

- Currently active on Twitter, LinkedIn, YouTube, blog

Source: Southern New Hampshire University website (http://www.snhu.edu/15863.asp)

SOCIAL QUOTES

On some presidents' fears of social media: "For some, [social media is] quite mechanical, it's just that they're not comfortable with technology and it's not what they do. Then, at the next level, you've got those who are comfortable with technology [but] not really comfortable with social media: 'I don't know how to do it,' 'I don't understand its conventions,' 'I fear that I may misstep,' and 'I'm not understanding how to be effective.' ... You have people who are in their jobs in some measure because they're so good at communications. Now, they're being asked to be effective in a venue where they don't really understand the underlying assumptions about etiquette, good communication. It's a more volatile space. If you are someone who is very careful and very measured, the kind of amplification and the way that things can go off track, the in-your-face quality of some of the criticism, can be a little daunting."

On being accessible to students: "Students have come to understand that if there's a problem that's not being addressed, they can come to my Twitter account, and it will be addressed almost immediately ... An hour later on Twitter ... you get all the kudos. All presidents live with some amount of political capital on their campuses, some amount of goodwill, and that bank can go up or down, and this is a way of adding to that bank if you manage it well."

On the perils of handing over the keys to your account: "Poorly done social media is worse than not doing it ... If you're a president having your campus PR people doing your social media account, it's almost like having an AOL account, it's like you might as well signal the world that you're completely out of date."

GREATEST SOCIAL TRAITS

Adaptable approach. LeBlanc is very much a chameleon in terms of his social media identity. He is able to appeal to diverse audiences by offering them a customized experience if they follow him on Twitter or through his blog. Like other presidents on social media, LeBlanc covers issues and advents in higher ed policy and decision-making, having carved out a nice little niche for himself in social media thought leadership circles, but also celebrates his institutional successes and puts an emphasis on providing customer service to students, too. What differentiates LeBlanc's approach from others is how deftly he is able to shift between content for each of these audiences while also ensuring he is not solely engaging in one-way communication. Flexibility in one's social media approach is a valuable tool for higher ed leaders, in that sticking to one form of storytelling might attract only one type of audience, but appealing to a diverse range of stakeholders means being flexible in one's content offerings. LeBlanc is most effective on social media when he demonstrates that adaptability in recognition of his multiple audiences.

Image sharer. Social media marketers, influencers, and users alike have come to recognize that image-based content attracts more clicks than text-based content, and LeBlanc, either knowingly or unknowingly, has embraced this philosophy. He often shares images from events he's attending on and off campus, an approach increasingly taken by higher ed leaders on social media, but also goes beyond that to include vacation photos, links to memes, viral videos, and other content that reflects his diverse areas of interest. Social media has always been conversational, but now more than ever, it is also visual, and individuals who offer their followers dynamic content tend to find that those followers are more loyal as a result. LeBlanc does an effective job of offering his followers visual access to what life is like within the SNHU community, but also goes beyond the campus's borders to tell a broader and more colorful story about his life and interests.

Connected leader. In our interview, LeBlanc talked about the "political capital" a president could gain on campus by being a responsive customer servant, and he lives that through his social media approach as well. LeBlanc is very responsive to students who raise issues to him via social media, taking action to acknowledge those issues immediately but also ensuring that once those issues are resolved, that too is acknowledged in the social media space. As a result of his quick and responsive social media tactics, he appears connected as a leader to his institution and its needs, even when he is off campus or traveling. Social media has enabled higher ed leaders to alter and ameliorate perceptions of their roles, influence, and impact within a college or university community. By connecting with stakeholders directly through social media, presidents are changing the stereotypical and unfounded narrative of the disconnected leader who sits alone surrounded by leather-bound books in the ivory tower. LeBlanc is part of a new breed of presidents who actively seek opportunities to connect with their stakeholders and effect meaningful change in their lives.

Chapter 13

—

#FollowTheLeader

In one of the final presidential interviews I conducted as part of my re-search, a Canadian college president raised an important issue with respect to his social media engagement efforts.

He spoke to the very real phenomenon of social networks coming and going, rising and falling in popularity. Examples of such networks include MySpace and Friendster, which had brief periods of wide-scale recognition and usage among mass audiences over a period of a couple of years, but struggled to maintain an active user base.

This president then asked: Given this volatile landscape of constantly fluctuating options in terms of social media technology, networks, chan-nels, and platforms, does a higher ed leader's approach to social media engagement even matter if the social network a president embraces could be abandoned in a matter of months? Is it really worth investing the time out of a president's busy schedule to embrace social media when it's such an unknown quantity?

Based on the results of my research, the answer to that question is ... com-plex.

We've certainly tried to take a stab at answering that and questions like it within this book, and the best we can tell you is this: It depends. The decision to embrace social media, if you're a higher ed leader, is a matter of weighing your personal tolerance for risk and what you perceive as the potential rewards of social media engagement.

Quite frankly, embracing any of the best practices recommended by this book is entirely a matter of personal preference. But perhaps you should consider the following as you make your decision.

There exists a contingent of college and university presidents across North America using social media to engage with their key stakeholders and to advance their personal, professional, and institutional interests. This emerg-ing group of higher ed leaders actively listens and responds to the feedback of students and other stakeholders within and outside of their institutions, and do so, frequently, by engaging in a visible, ongoing dialogue with those groups. They publicly celebrate institutional achievements such as athletic successes or research discoveries. They champion their institutions to influential constituencies, including government officials, alumni, and donors. They humanize themselves by sharing personal details about their lives and families, and they highlight the work they do away from their desks by updating anyone who will listen about the conferences, events, and meetings they attend as well as the relationships they manage in their role as president. These social-media-active college and university presidents share their personal and institutional stories with their most important stakeholders through social media, and that doesn't look to be changing any time soon.

These higher ed leaders use social media tools like Twitter, Facebook, LinkedIn, YouTube, Google+, Instagram, and blogs to engage with key constituencies, share details about their lives and work, gather intelligence about trends in their sector, and reach audiences they might not otherwise have the opportunity to connect with.

And yet business leadership researchers observe that many organizational senior leaders continue to struggle with weighing the perceived risks and opportunities that social media presents.

For a university or college president in particular, the decision of whether to "go social" involves weighing a number of costs and benefits and asking critical questions like these:

- If I make a public misstep on social media, what will the repercussions be to me and my institution?
- If my account is hacked, what damage could that do to me and my institution?
- Is my communications style suited to social media?

As we've discussed throughout this book, assessing your communication style, knowing your risk tolerance, and engaging in critical self-examination are just a couple of things you need to think about before engaging on social media.

We also discussed the opinion, held by many of the higher ed leaders I interviewed, that currently, it is not a necessity for a Canadian or American college or university president to engage with key stakeholders using social media. However, those same presidents added an important caveat about the not-too-distant future: that they expected social media literacy to be required learning for college and university presidents soon enough.

So, be aware that the tide is changing. Like email and the telephone before that, social media is on the rise (if it hasn't risen already).

As part of my research for this book, I came across the name of Sir William Preece, a 19th-century chief engineer with the British Postal Service, who is known, historically, for the following quotation: "The Americans have need of the telephone, but we do not. We have plenty of messenger boys." Preece's statement, reflecting his inability or unwillingness to see the potential of the telephone in 1876, is one higher ed leaders should take note of—not because failing to embrace social media will result in history recording a college or university president as a kind of 21st-century Luddite, but rather, because Preece denied the potential of the technology before even giving it fair consideration.

So, let me put this challenge to the readers of this book. Don't knock it until you try it. Mess around with a few social media platforms before you reject them outright. Only after giving them fair consideration can you truly be in an informed position to argue the merits or weaknesses of social media.

Perceptions of social media are changing, too. From higher ed leaders to the world's top senior executives, there is growing acceptance within the C-suites of many organizations of social media engagement as a valuable communications activity. According to a 2013 report by CEO.com, almost 32 percent of Fortune 500 CEOs have at least one profile on some social network, with the biggest growth happening on Twitter, LinkedIn, Google+, and Facebook. Notably, college and university presidents are way ahead of their Fortune 500 counterparts, with more than half of them on Facebook or Twitter, according to a 2013 University of Massachusetts Dartmouth study.

College and university presidents now operate in a landscape of tightened budgets and institutions competing tooth and nail for every student. With mounting data suggesting that the presence of higher ed leaders on social media could have the power to affect key institutional metrics such as recruitment and retention; to have a positive impact on personal, professional, and institutional reputations and interests; and to offer senior executives the chance to engage in new ways with important constituencies, I would argue that the question of necessity could be resolved sooner than any of us think.

Bonus Content

#QuestioningYourBarriers

More than anything else, studying best practices in the social media engagement of higher ed leaders has granted me a full appreciation of the specific complexities and challenges of the roles of college and university presidents. Others have expounded upon these complexities more effectively than I ever could. Livio Di Matteo, a Canadian economics professor, wrote in a 2012 blog post titled "What Is a University President Worth?" the following description, which I think encapsulates the multiple and intersecting demands of the position, in a North American context, pretty well:

> Being a university president is a pretty complex job. It is part diplomat, part fundraiser, part cheerleader, part civil service administrator, part strategic visionary, part financial planner, and part firefighter given the tendency for assorted crises to flare up. The main tasks are really forging community relationships (both internal and external to the university), fundraising for the university as its front man, and general strategic vision and direction. Day-to-day management of academic and financial affairs as well as dealing with the staff and faculty is usually the preserve of a vice president particularly at the larger places. The buck does eventually stop at the president, as she or he is ultimately accountable to the board.

The portfolio and its associated responsibilities are so expansive that Di Matteo's summary doesn't even specifically touch on all the accountabilities that higher ed leaders are faced with.

The 22 Canadian and American college and university presidents I interviewed as part of my research helped me to understand that some of them adopted social media because they seemed to have an innate understanding of the value of these channels as well as a genuine curiosity about them. And once they started using social media, they were hooked. But others had to decide whether they could afford to integrate social media into their already busy lives and assess whether the commitment was worthwhile. They also had to overcome barriers to entry. In other words, every college president I interviewed was active on social media despite the fact they had plenty of reasons not to be.

With very valid reasons to stay away from social media engagement, and even its supporters acknowledging that barriers to entry exist, why then do so many leaders disregard these barriers and launch social media accounts for themselves? Let's examine and address each perceived barrier one at a time.

DO I HAVE TIME FOR THIS?

Several of the presidents I interviewed noted that having an effective presence on social media, while worthwhile in terms of engaging key constituencies, was a major time commitment. This creates a challenge for leaders already struggling with having too much to do. One American college president told me, in reference to his day-to-day social media commitments, that "sometimes, it feels like we're being strategic, and other times it just feels like we're feeding the beast." Some leaders voiced the concern that their social media activities were, at times, a kind of "make-work" responsibility with little, if any, impact on personal, professional, or institutional interests.

Others, though, have found ways to work social media into their daily lives. For example, R. Bowen Loftin, the former president of Texas A & M and current chancellor of the University of Missouri, said:

> [Social media] doesn't really interfere with my other work, meetings I go to, paperwork I do ... I tend to take out time early in the morning or later in the afternoon or early evening ... I think people have to simply recognize if you're a public university president, your life is pretty open. This is just one more way it's open. It adds more risk by having one more vehicle or venue ... but that risk to me is well worth it to gain the interactivity I want with my students.

WHAT TOOLS SHALL I USE?

Beyond the real concern about the time commitment required to engage on social media, another barrier to entry was a lack of consensus on which platform(s) to embrace, due to the constantly evolving nature of social media technology and concern about how much reach various platforms had among constituents. One Canadian college president expressed his belief that a challenge for higher ed leaders in embracing social media engagement is the fear that they may choose the wrong tool to wield:

> I think the challenge right now is the platforms [presidents] choose to engage on are just changing so quickly ... it's the flavour of the day ... for a while, it was all about blogs, okay now it's Twitter, then it's Facebook, and now it's not Facebook. It's almost that you don't know which platform ultimately to settle on, and by the time you get one platform, your constituency's vacated it and they're off to another one.

A number of the presidents I interviewed agreed with this observation, saying that choosing a particular social media tool from among the ever-increasing number of options was a barrier to entry. It is also fascinating (and telling) to note that even though social networks continue to evolve and new ones spring up daily, the presidents interviewed for this research have chosen to continue their presence on certain social channels despite the rapid rate of change and the entry of new players into this space. They've focused primarily on established channels like their own blog, Facebook, Twitter, YouTube, LinkedIn, Google+, and the recently emerged Instagram—in short, those channels where they were likely to find a large number of their constituents already engaged.

Elizabeth Stroble, president of Webster University, prefers Twitter as her primary social media tool of choice but advises higher ed leaders not to get too caught up in the medium and instead focus on the message as well as active listening:

> Twitter suits my style of communication and community building quite well ... I pick pieces and parts of stories about our people, our places, and I spread them out for other members of our community to know. And then my other major communication role that I have taken on as president is translating our stories out to a larger world, whether it be alums or leaders in the communities, or possible donors, or thought leaders, so I'm getting our story out in ways that make it easier to reach those people. And then I'm scanning that external environment and learning more about public policy issues, leadership opportunities, ways that our internal community needs to not only respond but lead in partnership. Social media makes that very immediate and spontaneous and gives access to a wide range of perspectives, opinions, sources—and you can do it quickly without tremendous effort. For me, it's pure fun.

IS IT REALLY NECESSARY?

Yet another barrier highlighted by some interviewees was their own belief that, despite their personal social media engagement, there would be little in the way of repercussions or uproar if they left the platforms or had no presence whatsoever, since their institutions already possessed social media accounts that achieved similar or parallel objectives.

One Canadian college president told me that he didn't fear not having a presence on social media because it wasn't, in his eyes, a necessity, but rather, merely a preference: "If I drop off of social media, it's not going to lead to my peril or become a disadvantage for my institution because … my institution is active on social media … I think it's a preference." This president added that he believed maintaining a presence on social media was a personal choice for a higher ed leader. (In fact, data highlighting the comparative value of personal versus institutional social media accounts when it comes to senior leaders is a virtually unexplored area of research.)

By contrast, Paul LeBlanc, president of Southern New Hampshire University, said that ignoring evolving communications channels and technology may make it more difficult for higher ed leaders to engage with their key stakeholders:

> I don't know if [social media] is a necessity, but I think it's moving in that direction. If you look at the data on young people and how little they use email, for example, compared to social media, it really means that if you're not in that space, you're not having a conversation with them. And it's going to be a lot harder to reach them.

I JUST DON'T GET SOCIAL MEDIA

The next barrier identified by many of the presidents interviewed was a lack of familiarity with social media technology among older higher ed leaders. This lack of a comprehensive understanding about the tools, culture, conventions, opportunities, and risks was consistently listed as one of the biggest reasons certain college and university presidents in Canada and the United States had yet to fully embrace social media or were hesitant to adopt the technology.

Dominic Giroux, the 39-year-old head of Laurentian University, revealed in his interview that he believed there to be a correlation between the age of a senior executive and the willingness to embrace social media tools: "I think there may be an age factor here where [if] a president is in his 30s or early 40s, he'll feel more comfortable on social media … Someone who is in their 60s or 70s … may not." While some research acknowledges a potential knowledge gap experienced by organizational senior leaders with respect to their understanding of the uses and impact of social media tools, this perceived lack of understanding has not directly been correlated to the ages of the leaders in question.

WHAT IF I MAKE A PUBLIC MISSTEP?

Another significant factor emerging from the interviews (and my research) that highlighted barriers college and university presidents face in embracing social media was the fear of a costly misstep or a loss of control in terms of managing reputational issues. Many presidents stated their belief that higher ed presidents fear making a very public mistake on social media that could damage their own or their institution's reputations.

Paul LeBlanc told me that one of the challenges for higher ed leaders is accepting that social media is more volatile than other communications channels:

> You have people who are in their jobs in some measure because they're so good at communications. Now, they're being asked to be effective in a venue where they don't really understand the underlying assumptions about etiquette [and] good communication. It's a more volatile space. If you are someone who is very careful and very measured, the kind of amplification and the way that things can go off track, the in-your-face quality of some of the criticism, can be a little daunting for people.

According to recent history, some of these fears are warranted, with numerous examples of presidents on social media suffering reputational damage as a result of their real-world and social media missteps.

Even so, St. Francis Xavier University President Kent MacDonald, whom I interviewed while he was president of Algonquin College, said that in his view, the risks brought on by a higher ed leader making a misstep on social media were dwarfed by the potential opportunities and benefits:

> There's no doubt in my mind that using social media poses risk, but so does driving to work in the morning, launching new programs, and doing work in Saudi Arabia … It's a question of how do you manage that risk, and what is reasonable, and how risk tolerant you are … And I think the benefits that I accrue and the benefits our institution accrues greatly outweigh the risk.

WILL IT MAKE A DIFFERENCE?

Another barrier raised by some interviewees was the belief that their social media activities would not measurably contribute to the strategic interests of their institution. That is to say, how could they justify their presence on social media if they did not believe their activities contributed to the goals of their organization? A few of the higher ed leaders discussed the lack of metrics beyond "likes" and "followers" to evaluate the success of social media ventures, as well as tangible tools to measure correlation and causation between a president's presence on social media and advancement of institutional priorities.

Dillard University President Walter Kimbrough said that he believed a presidential social media account offered followers a perspective and content that they simply couldn't gain access to through an institutional account:

> I follow a good number of presidents ... I'm watching how they use it ... Talking about stories that they think students or their alums should read, stories about their institution, events on campus ... they use it as a promotional tool. Some ... will engage in more personal conversations on their Twitter feeds ... It's personality-driven, and a common theme is presidents realizing that this is a way to toot our horns about what's happening on our campuses, and even if we do it just for that ... to me, it's worth it ... It's a free way to pat people and the institution on the back.

Similarly, Scott Miller, president of Bethany College, said, "What I've found to be the value in it all has been with donors, corporations, and government leaders who follow me, who feel like they have that one-on-one relationship, and ... I can cultivate those constituents for a benefit-return for the institution, faster, as a result of the social media connection."

ULTIMATE VALUE

I want make it clear that my addressing of and responding to these individual social media barriers to entry is not an attempt on my part to obfuscate the very real concerns some higher ed leaders have about venturing into the social media landscape. As I have stated throughout this book, developing a presence on social media is a very personal decision—one that no one else can make for a college or university president.

For some readers, these barriers will continue to prevent them from embracing social media as a communications tool with which to engage institutional stakeholders, but I do think it's important to address the perceptions held by certain senior executives, and for them to hear from their colleagues and counterparts about why those barriers should not be considered insurmountable. A growing number of college and university presidents are weighing the benefits and risks, evaluating their perceived barriers to entry, and deciding social media is an emerging way to engage with their stakeholders.

#RisksAndRewards

Many of the higher ed leaders interviewed for this project revealed a number of different areas of perceived risk and opportunity when engaging as a senior leader on social media. These potential risks and opportunities were personal to each executive but spoke to the unquestioned importance of a college or university president understanding the repercussions of venturing into the social sphere.

PERCEIVED RISKS FOR HIGHER ED LEADERS

Some researchers argue that college or university presidents on social media are particularly exposed to risk because of the public-facing nature of their work. Five major types of risks were identified through the interviews conducted for this book, as follows:

1. Personal security. A small number of Canadian and American presidents interviewed highlighted their concern that their social media activities and updates, particularly those of a personal nature, including travel schedules, might be monitored by criminal elements who could take advantage of that information to commit crimes against themselves or their families. Little in the way of secondary research has either substantiated or discounted this risk, but actively sharing one's movements across social media certainly enables an individual to be tracked more closely.

2. Reputational damage. Almost all the higher ed leaders I spoke to as part of my research listed the fear of a publicly viewed misstep through their social media engagement as a going concern. The fear of saying the wrong thing in a tweet or Facebook post, or having something they have said misconstrued by other social media users and then becoming embroiled in a controversy that could damage a personal or institutional reputation, was highlighted as both a potential and very real threat to presidents operating in the space. One of the presidents who raised the issue of the risk of reputational damage also highlighted the fact that social media enables the opportunity to participate in a two-way discussion and potentially correct inaccurate comments. Similarly, one American college president pointed out that social media can be used to explain the "rationale" behind institutional decisions, and particularly for controversial decisions. The president stated that justifications for decisions were not always accepted on social media, but the acknowledgement of the differing viewpoint was appreciated by student stakeholders. However, research indicates that higher ed leaders

may not always be able to repair reputational damage by addressing controversy through their personal social media accounts.

3. Account security. Some presidents interviewed told me that another concern of theirs was their personal social media account being hacked, resulting in potential reputational damage to themselves and their institutions. Three of the 22 presidents interviewed made reference to personal experiences in which their Twitter and Facebook accounts were seized by hackers and unflattering messages were posted under their names. The damage from these instances would often be limited, but one college president described now having less confidence in the security protocols of certain social networks.

4. Alienating key stakeholder relationships. A majority of the higher ed leaders I spoke to as part of my research referenced a fear that their social media engagement could alienate key stakeholder relationships, including those with students, staff, faculty, and external constituencies. St. Francis Xavier University President Kent MacDonald, whom I interviewed while he was president of Algonquin College, said that higher ed leaders need to show a deft touch in their social media messaging, staying positive in their engagement as often as possible and not being lured into arguments that can be spun out of control:

> I need to be aware that if I go out using these tools too strongly that it could cause some embarrassment to our college ... Just simply being aware that people read it and it can cause harm as much as it can cause good things to happen.

The higher ed leaders I spoke to once again said this risk is very much tied to the concern about making a public misstep. The potential for this to take place increases significantly when or if a senior leader approaches social media activities recklessly.

5. Negative impact on institutional interests. The biggest going concern for the presidents I interviewed was a fear that their public missteps on their personal accounts could harm institutional interests. A negative impact could take the form of lowered rankings by respected publications or reputational damage for their institutions. R. Bowen Loftin, in reference to his former role as president of Texas A & M, argued that his mitigation strategy was an approach to social media communication that emphasized mindfulness and thoughtful discourse:

> I'm a public official ... I run a public university ... That's just my life, so you live in a fishbowl as a president anyway, and any

president who is going to survive even a month in office has to be extremely aware … that what they do is public in almost every way … And that should drive what you say and what you do in any kind of electronic communication.

Meanwhile, researchers and communications consultants alike recommend a similar approach to social media engagement for organizational leaders, namely, approaching all communications from the perspectives of the audiences disseminating that information.

REAL AND POTENTIAL OPPORTUNITIES GAINED

Higher ed leaders that I interviewed also revealed that they believed their social media activities offered themselves and their institutions particular rewards, benefits, and opportunities. These findings are in keeping with academic research that suggests that social media usage can help institutions advance their interests and even boost key organizational metrics. Interviewees identified five major types of opportunities gained through their personal usage of social media tools.

1. Intelligence gathering. A small number of the presidents interviewed mentioned they believed one of the greatest opportunities that social media engagement gave them was the chance to monitor what internal and external key stakeholders and competitors were communicating and promoting through those channels and to gather competitive intelligence. As one American university president explained:

> By being on social media, one of things I do is regularly use a fair number of social media search engines to look for references to the university … I've been able to find references to the university that have been good or positive … and then I will jump in on social media … it's that extra touch that adds a bit of a personal element to it for somebody I would never have found otherwise or never have interacted with otherwise.

Some researchers have highlighted the importance for college and university presidents on social media to follow key constituencies before engaging to gain an understanding of the types of content that may be most effective for individual and institutional purposes.

2. Thought leadership. Four of the presidents interviewed for this study made the case that social media engagement could help a college or university president become recognized as a thought leader, if the president used that platform to share dynamic and interesting content that

sparked and provoked discourse and encouraged further discussion from other higher ed thought leaders. While three of the presidents cited blogging in this context, another talked about using Twitter to find and promote thought leadership content. One president in particular referenced the usage of social media not only to share thought leadership stories but also learn about them. President Scott Miller of Bethany College talked about how social media enabled him to participate and lead discussions with his counterparts on topics ranging from higher ed policy and technology to the future of postsecondary education. Similarly, President Elizabeth Stroble of Webster University highlighted how she used her presence on Twitter to actively monitor conversations from other thought leaders to identify ways she could enhance her own leadership and the strategies employed by her institution. Another American college president appreciated the fact that social media allowed for opportunities to learn about public policy issues and leadership approaches, and that all of this learning and sharing could happen in real time without much effort. Other research supports the notion that social media can be used to promote, share, and drive thought leadership content by organizational leaders.

3. Strengthened reputation. Some college and university presidents mentioned their belief that social media engagement by a higher ed leader could boost personal, professional and institutional reputations. Kent MacDonald argued there was a very real link between communicating using social media tools and becoming recognized as a leading postsecondary institution:

> For me personally, I'm not satisfied until our college is considered Canada's preeminent polytechnic institution ... [Social media is] not everything, but it certainly helps what we're trying to do as a college. Is it personally essential? No. But I think there's a correlation between being an effective president and ... social media tools.

While research into the tangible impact of social engagement is ongoing, little work has been done in higher education circles around the tangible measurement of reputational and institutional benefits of usage by college and university presidents.

4. New and enhanced strategic relationships. A number of the presidents I interviewed referred to the potential of social media engagement by higher ed leaders to build and strengthen strategic relationships with internal and external partners. Dillard University President Walter Kimbrough noted that social media tools are particularly effective in forming bonds with stakeholders who might otherwise be difficult to reach:

> For most presidents, it's about talking about how I want to use social media, how can I be strategic in my usage ... how do we use this as an advancement tool, how does this advance the institution, broaden our exposure, reach our influencers, those we want to influence, potential students, parents ...

Many of the Canadian and American higher ed presidents I spoke to had already reported using social media tools to communicate with key stakeholders and discuss institutional issues and interests. President Tom Thompson of Olds College described how he used social media engagement to form a strategic relationship with an Alberta government official that helped to boost his institution's funding:

> It would be fair to say that I have an uncommon relationship with our Minister of Enterprise and Advanced Education as a direct function of us communicating through Twitter. We have a 40-something-year-old minister ... who has an advanced education, and he is also the deputy premier of the province, and he has an obsession with using Twitter. If you know that to be true, as a president, and if you are worth your salt, in terms of the development, maintaining, and nurturing of external relationships, that would in turn convert into influence, you would want to take advantage of that fact and to develop and nurture that relationship via social media. That relationship has in turn spawned direct facial meeting contact and influenced initiatives, projects, and developments. And now is influencing the allocation of resources.

Other research highlights the strengthening of strategic relationships as a potential benefit for organizational leaders and CEOs active on social media.

5. Positive impact on institutional interests. By far the biggest opportunity, either realized or unrealized, identified by the presidents I interviewed was the potential to advance institutional interests through presidential social engagement. One American college president stated that social media was part of the institution's student success strategy and that communication on social networking channels was important in times of both stability and controversy. This president also made the argument that the value of social media with respect to developing strategic relationships with media and donors was clear. The power of social media engagement by higher ed senior leadership to drive institutional interests has also been supported by both academic and industry-based research.

A President's Cheat Sheet

Account security: Higher ed leaders have and will continue to face risks with respect to the security of their social media accounts. There have been a number of cases, particularly in the United States, of college and university presidents' personal social media accounts being hacked, resulting in reputational damage to themselves and their institutions. The damage caused by these situations is often limited and isolated, but it can shake your confidence in the security protocols of certain social networks. Be sure to regularly change your social media password(s), check privacy settings, and be careful about who has access to your social media profiles.

Institutional account: This is the social media presence of your institution, which might share content about your campus's news, events, and achievements and other announcements. Often operated by dedicated staff, the institutional social media account serves a different purpose than a presidential one does. An institutional account often focuses more intently on storytelling and information sharing rather than two-way engagement, conversation with stakeholders, relationship building, and advancement of institutional interests.

Intelligence gathering: One of the unique opportunities that social media tools present to higher ed leaders is the chance to actively listen to and monitor what internal and external stakeholders and competitors are communicating and promoting to their networks and to gather competitive intelligence. You should follow key constituencies before engaging to gain an understanding of the types of content that may be most effective for individual and institutional purposes.

Personal choice: A higher ed leader must personally choose whether to engage on social media. If you decide to proceed, ideally it should be out of a sincere desire to tell institutional and personal stories, connect with key stakeholders, and advance your institution's strategic objectives. You ought not commit to a presence on social media if you have little belief in its power to benefit you or your campus or if you believe it will only serve to harm your own and your institutional reputations.

Presidential presence: This is the presence of a college or university president, located on any number of social media channels, most often operated by the president personally with support from strategic advisers and communications staff. You must make a personal choice whether to pursue a presence on social media. Some have argued that such a presence can serve to advance institutional objectives through engagement with key stakeholders as well as demonstrate a senior leader's connectedness with the campus community.

President's blog: A president's blog is a platform through which you can share long-form stories, opinion pieces, or announcements in your own words. This website or webpage is often launched by the Office of the President or the president personally at a college or university. Most blogs allow readers to post either moderated or unmoderated comments in response.

Role model: A role model is an individual on social media who engages with stakeholders and shares content in a way that you consider particularly effective. It's useful to search for social media role models among your peers before establishing your own account(s). While it is not recommended to mimic a role model exactly, you should identify the key strategies that person employs effectively and attempt to apply those practices to your own personal social media engagement.

Rules of engagement: Your rules of engagement for social media interactions reflect the subject area and content you will or will not share and discuss while engaging on social media. You should develop your own personal rules of engagement, seeking input, where appropriate, from strategic advisers, public relations professionals, and social-media-active counterparts. It is important to note that your social media rules of engagement are personal to you and should be respected by your strategic advisers.

Social media strategy: Developed in association with a strategic adviser or communications staff, your social media strategy serves as a guiding document for your social media engagement to ensure your activities align with institutional goals. It typically contains objectives, supporting resources, measurement tools, crisis readiness plans, content and event schedules, and recommended tactics.

Two-way engagement: An essential element of social-media-based communication, two-way engagement is the back-and-forth exchange of ideas, content, and conversation among users on any social media platform. Higher ed leaders must be prepared to embrace two-way engagement if they choose to establish their presence on any social network.

Viral: This term refers to the phenomenon of a story, comment, video, or image being shared and widely spread across social networks, sometimes in a matter of minutes, hours, or days. Some higher ed leaders may not be accustomed to the speed with which stories, both positive and negative, can go viral on social media. You need to be mindful of the risks and opportunities of viral content. If social media users catch wind of a controversy, they have the opportunity not only to spread the story to their own personal networks and those of followers, but also to comment on the story with their own views and feedback, which could pose some reputational risks. Similarly, positive stories or content could go viral, which might boost reputational perceptions of you or your institution.

Volatility: A reality of operating in the social media landscape is the volatility of the various networks and platforms. Higher ed leaders must thoughtfully consider all content they share on social media and recognize the potential implications of doing so. Opinions and information shared on social media, for better or worse, are considered public, and you must be prepared for individuals with strong and, at times, uninformed opinions who may respond quickly or aggressively to what you have to say. Due to the fast-paced and informal nature of social media, positions and statements can be misconstrued or misinterpreted, which is why caution is advised regarding what you choose to share on social media.

Bibliography

Ashford, E. (2013, August 20). Social media help college presidents reach new audiences. *Community College Daily*. Retrieved from http://www.ccdaily.com/Pages/Campus-Issues/Social-media-help-college-president-reach-new-audiences.aspx. Short url: mstnr.me/FTLref1.

Barnes, N., & Lescault, A. (2013, August). College Presidents Out-Blog and Out-Tweet Corporate CEO's. University of Massachusetts Dartmouth Center for Marketing Research. Retrieved from http://www.umassd.edu/cmr/socialmediaresearch/collegepresidentsoutblog/. Short url: mstnr.me/FTLref4.

Barrows, C. (2014, March 28). Social Talk: President Santa Ono. Retrieved from http://medium.com/@cbarrows/social-talk-president-santa-ono-8a5129b8786a. Short url: mstnr.me/FTLref2.

Bradshaw, J. (2012, November 19). Who Canadian universities need now. *Globe and Mail*. Retrieved from http://www.theglobeandmail.com/news/national/education/who-canadian-universities-need-now/article5461489. Short url: mstnr.me/FTLref3.

Cherenson, M. (2009, August 18). Public relations is leading social media engagement [Forum post]. *PRSAY*. Retrieved from http://prsay.prsa.org/index.php/2009/08/18/public-relations-is-leading-social-media-engagement. Short url: mstnr.me/FTLref5.

Church, E. (2010, September 1). From the ivory tower to the Facebook wall. *Globe and Mail*. Retrieved from http://www.theglobeandmail.com/life/parenting/back-to-school/from-the-ivory-tower-to-the-facebook-wall/article1315249. Short url: mstnr.me/FTLref6.

Crowell, G. (2012, April 9). Can PR support thought leadership? (Or are they mutually exclusive?) [Blog post]. Sword and the Script. Retrieved from http://www.swordandthescript.com/2012/04/can-pr-support-thought-leadership-or-are-they-mutually-exclusive/. Short url: mstnr.me/FTLref8.

Davis III, C. H. F., Deil-Amen, R., Rios-Aguilar, C., & González Canché, M. S. (2012). *Social media in higher education: A literature review and research directions*. Retrieved from http://academia.edu/1220569/Social_Media_in_Higher_Education_A_Literature_Review_and_Research_Directions/. Short url: mstnr.me/FTLref9.

Di Matteo, L. (2012, March 24). What is a university president worth? [Blog post]. *Worthwhile Canadian Initiative*. Retrieved from http://worthwhile.typepad.com/worthwhile_canadian_initi/2012/03/what-is-a-university-president-worth.html. Short url: mstnr.me/FTLref10.

Falls, J. (2008, July 18). Social media is the responsibility of public relations [Blog post]. *Social Media Explorer*. Retrieved from http://www.socialmediaexplorer.com/online-public-relations/social-media-is-the-responsibility-of-public-relations/. Short url: mstnr.me/FTLref11.

Groysberg, B., & Slind, M. (2012, June). Leadership is a conversation. *Harvard Business Review*. Retrieved from http://hbr.org/2012/06/leadership-is-a-conversation/ar/pr/. Short url: mstnr.me/FTLref12.

Grunig, J. E. (2009). Paradigms of global public relations in an age of digitalisation. *Prism*, 6(2). Retrieved from http://www.prismjournal.org/fileadmin/Praxis/Files/globalPR/GRUNIG.pdf. Short url: mstnr.me/FTLref13.

Hager, M. (2013, June 4). UBC president Stephen Toope doubles down on his dislike for Twitter. *Vancouver Sun*. Retrieved from http://www.vancouversun.com/technology/president%20Stephen%20Toope%20doubles%20down%20dislike%20Twitter/8479673/story.html. Short url: mstnr.me/FTLref14.

Hanstein, A. (2013, June 4). The voice of college presidents on social media. *Community College Times*. Retrieved from http://www.communitycollegetimes.com/Pages/Campus-Issues/Presidents-take-to-social-media.aspx. Short url: mstnr.me/FTLref15.

Kiley, K. (2013, April 12). Who's in charge? University presidents work to increase recognizability. *Inside Higher Ed*. Retrieved from http://www.insidehighered.com/news/2013/04/12/university-presidents-work-increase-recognizability-alumni. Short url: mstnr.me/FTLref16.

Kolowich, S. (2011, May 3). College presidents around USA impersonated on Twitter. *USA Today*. Retrieved from http://usatoday30.usatoday.com/news/education/2011-04-18-college-presidents-impersonated-twitter.htm. Short url: mstnr.me/FTLref17.

Leaders' lack of social media savvy holding firms back. (2013, March 27). *Human Resource Management Online*. Retrieved from http://www.hrmonline.ca/hr-news/leaders-lack-of-social-media-savvy-holding-firms-back-173635.aspx. Short url: mstnr.me/FTLref18.

Levick, R. (2012, November 27). Social media and the boardroom: Critical questions directors need to ask. *Fast Company*. Retrieved from http://www.fastcompany.com/3003393/social-media-and-boardroom-critical-questions-directors-need-ask. Short url: mstnr.me/FTLref19.

Paul, R. (2011). *Leadership Under Fire: The Challenging Role of the Canadian University President*. Quebec: McGill-Queen's University Press.

Perry, C. (2013, May 29). Research: Social media finally seen as essential for CEOs. *Forbes*. Retrieved from http://www.forbes.com/sites/chrisperry/2013/05/29/research-social-media-finally-seen-as-essential-for-ceos. Short url: mstnr.me/FTLref20.

Quotations by Author Sir William Preece. (n.d.). *The Quotations Page*. Retrieved from http://www.quotationspage.com/quotes/Sir_William_Preece. Short url: mstnr.me/FTLref21.

Samuel, A. (2012, April 2). Better leadership through social media. *Wall Street Journal*. Retrieved from http://online.wsj.com/article/SB10001424052970203753704577255531558650636.html. Short link: http://mstnr.me/FTLref22.

Stoner, M. (2012, April 19). Why college presidents aren't more social. mStoner.com blog. Retrieved from http://www.mstoner.com/blog/uncategorized/why_college_presidents_arent_more_social/. Short url: mstnr.me/FTLref23.

Stoner, M. (2012, November 1). A quick-start guide to social media for college and university presidents [Blog post]. *CASE*. Retrieved from http://blog.case.org/2012/11/01/a-quick-start-guide-to-social-media. Short url: mstnr.me/FTLref24.

Walgrove, A. (2012, April 16). What college presidents can gain from tweeting. *Huffington Post*. Retrieved from http://www.huffingtonpost.com/amanda-walgrove/college-president-twitter_b_1428873.html. Short url: mstnr.me/FTLref25.

Walsh, K. (2012, October 28). Can social media play a role in improving retention in higher education? Research says it can [Blog post]. *EmergingEdTech*. Retrieved from http://www.emergingedtech.com/2012/10/can-social-media-play-a-role-in-improving-retention-in-higher-education-research-says-it-can. Short url: mstnr.me/FTLref26.

Young, J. (2011, May 1). A college unfriends its social-networking president. *The Chronicle of Higher Education*. Retrieved from http://chronicle.com/article/A-College-Unfriends-Its/127334. Short url: mstnr.me/FTLref27.

Zets, A. (2013, April 23). Why senior executives are resisting social media. *Social Media Today*. Retrieved from http://www.socialmediatoday.com/content/why-senior-executives-are-resisting-social-media. Short url: mstnr.me/FTLref28.

ABOUT THE AUTHOR

Dan Zaiontz is a Toronto-based professional communicator with more than eight years of diverse experience representing some of Canada's largest media brands. Including stints at Rogers Sportsnet and Canada's Olympic Broadcast Media Consortium, Dan has helped to share the stories of a number of major events and properties from the Vancouver 2010 Olympic Winter Games to the Toronto Blue Jays. In recent years, Zaiontz has pursued new public relations opportunities in the postsecondary education sector, joining the communications and strategic planning team at Seneca College, serving previously as the college's Sports Information and Promotions Coordinator and currently as Special Projects Coordinator and Professor. Specializing in social media strategy, speechwriting, and public relations, he completed a Master of Communications Management (MCM) from McMaster University–Syracuse University in 2014. Dan loves to talk about leadership, politics, the frustrations of being a Toronto sports fan, health foods, running, motivation, great TV and film (see: Aaron Sorkin), rock music (see: Foo Fighters), and ethical shopping (see: bleeding heart). Dan resides just north of Toronto with his wife, Rebecca, and their daughter, Samantha.

He can be reached on Twitter: **@danzaiontz.**

CPSIA information can be obtained at www.ICGtesting.com
Printed in the USA
LVOW05s1019100115

422129LV00003B/3/P

9 780988 878822